# My Enemy is a Coward

## Fighting an Enemy That You Can't See

Hiekaleez

*Our mission is to efficiently provide the world's finest, most comprehensive book publishing
service, enabling every author to experience success. To find out how to publish your book, your
way, and have it available worldwide, visit us online at www.trafford.com*

*Trafford rev. 4/5/2010*

 www.trafford.com

**North America & international**
toll-free: 1 888 232 4444 (USA & Canada)
phone: 250 383 6864 ♦ fax: 812 355 4082

# What's Inside

# My Enemy is a Coward: Fighting an Enemy That You Can't See

--Hiekaleez--

*North Carolina Central University – 1910 – 2010
Soaring on the Legacy "Celebrating 100 Years of
Truth and Service" Founded by James E. Shepard*

# PROLOGUE

We are all born for a reason. We have purpose and potential. The belief in the theory of predestination I have come to develop in my psyche. Predestination is the theory that each one of our lives is already determined. You may live your entire life and never figure out what your purpose for being here is. You may not have even gotten the opportunity to try for it. You can be educated, happy, and successful, but it is still possible that you haven't fulfilled your destiny. Sometimes life and its circumstances have a way of pulling you away from or pushing you towards fulfilling your purpose here on Earth. There may have been just this feeling that you have always had or maybe there's something that you were always good at and didn't know why! Just think. That may be the thing you were born for.

This is my story about my battle with this coward disease called Multiple Sclerosis. It has been a life changing journey that awakened this dreamer. The nightmare of carrying "this thing" came into my life at a time that I felt like I was on my way to making a positive impact in the world. Having Multiple Sclerosis (which I refer to as "this thing") interrupted **my** plans and led me to seek God and **His** plans for my life. This ended up being a great thing really. What the enemy meant for bad, through my Savior Jesus Christ, turned into the thing that will ultimately guide me into being a blessing to someone else. This is just what it took for me to look to fulfill my purpose! This cannot all be kept to myself. I figured out how I will win. By fighting with faith!

When a boy is very young, he might dream about things like being a policeman, a lawyer, a professional athlete, a musician, and the list goes on and on. As he grows older and reality sets in, his dreams may begin to change a little. He may begin to narrow down what he dreamed when younger- realizing his possibilities as well as his impossibilities. With faith all things are possible through Jesus Christ is what I believe. The concept that learning was just something a person must do while in this place called "Earth" was taught to me very early. You see for me early on in life I had this feeling that this wasn't my home. My physical address was known, but that's not the address I'm talking about. For some reason things always felt as if I was in a dream or something. Life just didn't seem real to me. As one grows older these things begin to look different to some people. You see, the *Bible* says in 1 Corinthians 13:11 that when a child you speak, think, and act as a child, but as you become of age you put away such childish things. Well, some of us don't.

For me that was the case. My dream of becoming a professional athlete changed to maybe becoming a professor or at least an educator of some kind. Growing up it was being an athlete and student that had begun to shape my identity. Playing little league baseball started the athlete in me up and it was my family that let me know early in life that being a good student came first. For me not doing my best wasn't an option. When I was about three years old, I saw my mom graduate from high school. Witnessing this led me to conclude that later in my life, that would be me. Being a good student would one day pay off for me. Now all the *Sesame Street, Reading Rainbow*, my grandma reading to me at night, and the buying of all this learning stuff began to make sense. Not even to mention all the cartoons and toys I fell in love with to help feed my imagination, which is healthy for a little child. I grew up in the housing projects of Scotland Neck, North Carolina. It was back then that the decision that this was not all that life has to offer dawned on me. Even as a little boy my dreams were big. There had to be more! This was the way I thought in the past when I was just a child.

I went from this little boy into a well polished dreamer and still dream to this day! Because of circumstances, some beyond my control, life for me would become somewhat bittersweet. In my high school, Southeast Halifax High School, there was somewhat of a town rivalry between two towns; Enfield, North Carolina and the town in which I am from

Scotland Neck, North Carolina. Most of the people that were involved didn't even realize that they were probably related to half of their foes, but some of my best friends to this day are from the town of Enfield. The bond between us began the summer before even starting high school in football training. From then on we all found our common ground and never became involved with all of the fighting, well most of us anyway. What kept us focused were our academics and athletics.

Participating in athletics alone wasn't enough for me. I was fortunate enough to become an exceptional student-athlete. I never wanted to be "just average." This fact would help me become a man later. Until this day those two things, athletics and school, are what we talk about all the time. Our coaches did tell us that would be the case for most of us. We depended on each other for a lot of things. Our friendships extended past the football field. In high school I played varsity football for three out of the four years there. For three years straight, beginning sophomore year, the prestigious opportunity to be named all-conference in football was bestowed upon me. In my senior year the class elected me to represent them as class president with my best female friend at the time being the vice-president. Honestly, to me she would have been better for the president job though. It was to my surprise that a 1070 was what my S.A.T score was after taking the test only once. Maybe it was the S.A.T Prep Class taken under Mrs. V. Robinson that year? Or it could have been all of those books read throughout my life that played a major role in all of this. That S.A.T score along with other skills earned me a full scholarship. It was a tough process, but in my senior year the North Carolina Teaching Fellows Scholarship to North Carolina Central University was awarded to me. I became an N.C.C.U high flying Eagle. Right then it should have been evident to me that I was blessed.

Like lots of people in a new environment, I had to adapt. It was taught to me in school somewhere that man will adapt to their environment. We somewhat have to or we miss out or get left behind. College for me was difficult. It wasn't the class work. But it was just everything else that was part of being a college student. Most of the time money was an issue for me. Semester refund checks were my main source of income, so lots of fun things that some of my friends did I couldn't do. Doing the best that you can with the little you got was how things always went with me anyway.

That meant sacrificing a lot of fun college experiences to make it through. There were two times that I fell in love and dealt the best I could with that, being that there wasn't a dad around to teach me better. My pockets wouldn't allow me to do lots of things with or for them. Those girls must have loved me for me. December 13, 2002 was my graduation day. I finished college with a Bachelor of Arts degree in History with a concentration in Education. That day I felt like I was on my way to achieving my dream.

The joy of graduating college came to a pause because the day after Christmas of the same year, my body had begun to change. I suffered a series of muscle spasms, which were very frightening to me. On January 5, 2003 I was in the hospital for the first time in my life. I was scared, but couldn't show fear because of not wanting my family to be scared for me. Then the hospital did a spinal tap, MRI, and the scary HIV test. My doctor concluded that it was because of Multiple Sclerosis (MS) that my body did this. It felt like a terrible joke was being played on me.

I must admit, my first reaction was like, "damn, something else to fight with!"

Already having to deal with coming out of my "never having money" and other things phase and now this! I felt like screaming because it really didn't seem fair to me! This changed my life dramatically. For a moment I was mad as hell, but there was no one around to blame. Being violent was not in my character, but if MS was a person I would put a hit out on him. My life would never be the same.

In the very beginning physically everything visible was fine then things began to change. Not long after my first hospital visit came my second visit. Eventually my plans to teach in North Carolina and then move far away were altered. "This thing" called MS is a coward because it won't show its face and it has been so frustrating for me.

The first year consisted of me being admitted into the hospital every three months for three visits to the hospital, and then it began to taper off. I wrote poems in my journals to counsel me. Crying to my paper using my pen as my eyes and the ink as my tears helped me to cope with this change in my life. Writing my feelings down drastically helped me, because the pen and paper wouldn't tell anyone how scared I really was. How more unsure of my future I had become! I just couldn't figure things out! I didn't sell drugs, curse people out or just make babies for the hell of it or anything. So I really didn't understand why this was happening to me!

When I was alone I cried out saying, Why me!? Why now!?

Something happened in September of that year in the midst of me going through a state of depression. A good friend of mine had me to call this person who I had never laid eyes on. She was a prophetess and after that phone call, my life took the best turn ever! No, she didn't heal me, but she guided me into a life that I would never regret.

Soon I would begin to be weaned away from the way in which I was feeling and living. After she prophesied for me, the decision to give my life to God wasn't hard at all. I realized that it really wasn't "my life" to give and that everything had already been given to me by Him anyway! My entire life my eyes had been "open wide shut." In spite of all of my wrongs He blessed and loved me anyway. The battle is not mine. God's got it! It's by His stripes that I am healed (Is 53:5). Now that my eyes had been opened, my fears slowly began to fade away. My problems seemed to be smaller than they appeared before. Through my faith in God all of my enemies were already defeated even if they can't be seen!

The fight with the enemy that can't be seen will continue until I go back home and leave this place. Let me correct that, because He told me to cast my cares on Him, and He will sustain me (Psalm 55:22) and fight my battles. While here I will just do my best to honor Him with my spirit and my faith. "MS" does have a face and that's why this book is being written. This book is for those who have Multiple Sclerosis or any other circumstance that may cause them to feel like giving up. It is to show them that "we can do it in spite of!"

This journey has been an interesting ride so far and it has just begun. I still got a ways to go, but I have to keep holding on tight! I refuse to let go, because you see for me the best is yet to come. In this book I intend to let my guard down a little; and let you in on why I think and act the way I do. Come and go with me on this journey into a little bit of "Hieke's" mind.

This is from my journals which took on the role as being my therapy. My enemy is a coward and I am writing to show that this, too, will pass! What God has set in motion can't be stopped!

# "The Best is Yet to Come"

When you are tired and
You feel like giving in
Just hold on tight to the Lord
Cause the enemy won't win

Know that the Lord is on your side
And you've already won
Stick to what you believe
The best is yet to come

I know right now
God seems to be ignoring you
But a test is going on, so pray
And Jesus will see you through!

Hold on I tell ya, do it
With all your might
If your grip is weak, regrip!
This time hold on tight.

Don't let go till tha end
God's not done
Just remember what He said
The best is yet to come!

*--Hiekaleez--*

# Chapter One

# Something Is Happening

I T WAS MY LAST SEMESTER in college and up to this point in my life there really hasn't been a health issue. My mom did tell me that as a baby I had a serious ear infection, but I don't remember it. There were a few head injuries over time though. One time was in the fifth grade while playing ball with some friends, I somehow managed to hit myself in the head with a baseball bat. There were stitches put near my right eye close to my temple for that. My face was swollen, but eventually it healed. Then there was this car accident back in college, which wasn't my fault. My forehead did hit the windshield and an ambulance took me to get checked at Duke Hospital in Durham, NC. The only thing that was wrong was that my forehead had been scarred from the collision. The last time that I even had a incident that put my body in harm was when this coward came from behind and hit me in the head by surprise. I guess he thought that I had something to do with an inner-town dispute between the guys from my side of town and his. Doctors at the hospital gave me stitches on my eye that time, but as usual, the wound healed.

One day during my last semester in college, I was heading up some long stairs coming from my dorm on my way to my 10:00 class. My body just wouldn't work for me. My foot kept getting hung on the steps. I just thought to myself, "I was too high up the steps to turn back now." The thought of turning back scared me because first of all, I would miss class. And secondly, I might lose my balance and fall back down those steps! "Hurting myself and falling would be very embarrassing," I thought. My school did have a 21 to 1 male to female ratio! How much and how soon swallowing my pride and shaking off humiliation ahead was unknown by me.

Initially I just assumed that what was going on with me was from my football days and that this too would just pass. Playing sports never caused me to be seriously injured and up until this point, my health had not been an issue. The earlier head injuries never showed any threatening signs to my future health either! Something was happening or had already happened! The thing was that I really didn't know which one it was!

About two weeks later when I was home from school for the weekend, it happened again. My body just seemed to have a mind of its own! My crew and I were walking and the more we walked, the further I got behind. They were leaving me! My instruction to them was to, "Go ahead." The place where they were headed was no mystery to me anyway. We were going to a friend's house because some girls were going there to just hang out. At that time what I really needed was a ride, but I just kept walking along the best I could. Walking had never before been so difficult!

Eventually I caught up with the guys, but my mind was trying to figure out why in the hell keeping up with them was so hard for me!? At that time the only thing that crossed my mind was maybe it was something from playing football that I played in the past. When I caught up with the guys, my mind wasn't even on the females that were at the place that we ended up. At that time focusing on them really wasn't on my mind. First of all, my body was just so tired. Secondly, my mind was still trying to figure out what was going on with me!

After awhile my cousin "Snap" drove up. Seeing him had never before excited me so much. I felt relieved and knew that when he left, I would be on that car no Matter where he was headed! It was Saturday night and just chilling was on my mind. After-all it was my weekend home from college! Eventually he did leave and sure enough I was on that car. The house we ended up to was the house of some of his boys.

Those guys were also cool with me, but there was something surprising that came up. We were in their sitting room, smoking some weed (marijuana), playing the video game, and just joking with a few other guys. Just like that my Saturday, the most important part of the weekend to me, had been spoiled!

Everything was good until some guys came from the back room. They must have overheard laughter coming from the sitting room. Eventually just hanging and tripping out with the fellas, had helped me to just stop the worrying and perk up. While there, I was just talking about the way that my body had been acting. One of the guys that came from the back room said something very stupid to me. He was high off cocaine and tried to comfort me. He offered me some and suggested that trying some of that would maybe help my body to act right. He just broke my good mood. Yes, the way that my body was acting did have me stressed, but trying that stuff was off limits for me! It wouldn't help, but it could create more problems! When we were younger he was my friend, but he had lost me because of that bad advice. Any respect that I had for him was gone just like that! Just think had my response have been to give me some, he probably would have! At the time smoking marijuana was already wrong for me to do, but damn he should have never come out of his mouth like that to me. At the time he thought he was helping me, but his problem actually was bigger than mine.

With all that had happened that night, I still was determined to chill as long as I didn't have to walk far. Back then, that was all that was on my agenda for the weekend. I was born on a Saturday, so Saturdays were dedicated to me having fun! The people that I was affiliated with were the "in-people" too. We were the people that were expected to be just "in the mix." Most of the guys I was around were hustlers or at least had money. That wasn't the case for me though, but most of them respected me and for the most part I reciprocated that to them. That entire evening seemed to be so long.

The next morning the problems with my body the night before were gone so it was really off of my mind. I went back to school that day and physically things seemed fine. It was back to going to class as usual trying to make this semester my last. I was already late graduating, because certain things had happened and my grades were just below my expectations. My G.P.A had to be at least a 3.0 when I graduated. That was just my personal goal. Graduation was about two months away and my grades were back to where they were supposed to be. After receiving my degree, it would be my time to continue on with the next phase in my life. The thought of being scared and facing "reality" didn't come up. My happiness and relief overpowered my fear. The only thing was that there was no more hiding behind being "a student" anymore. For so long being in school was my cover. It gave me an excuse to not face this world.

For a long time I hid behind this mask of being a "good little boy." I learned how to avoid trouble and not get caught, that's all. It just so happened that just "being me," whatever that meant, had gotten me this far. The only things that made me feel normal were academics and athletics. They both had become my passions. They were the two things that identified me. There had been no athletics for quite some time by now and very, very soon there'd be no more school to hide behind. My family had come to witness me graduate, but there was no party, no awards, no money, no car, etc. waiting for me back home. Out of all the hustlers and people with dough that I was around, when I was home from school, none of them even thought about that. There was this one girl, in line with me at graduation that told me that back at home where she was from in Maryland, her folks had a condo, a car, and a celebration just waiting for her! "Sure would be nice if someone did something like that for me," is what I thought to myself!

At the time my family just couldn't afford it, being that Christmas was so close. To me none of that mattered anyway. My baby sister, bless her heart, gave me five dollars to get something to eat with. I'll never forget that day. It was cold and raining! The idea of having to leave the girl that I loved behind in Durham to finish school, made graduating kind of "bitter-sweet" for me. What was mine that nobody could take away from me was my Bachelor of Arts Degree in History. Saturday, December 13, 2002 would become the day that meant another phase ended for me and a new one had begun. I wasn't ready for the life that very soon would be my new reality. The way that I had been raised was to be tough, but soon my strength would be tested in a way that really wasn't part of my plan.

Christmas was basically here and then a new year. The next thing that would take place in my life was really a surprise to me. Actually "this thing" changed my life. On December 26, 2003, the very next day after Christmas, something happened with my body that really "shook" me! Heading into this guy's house to chill with some friends my body just locked up. I had just gotten out of a van with two of my friends smoking some marijuana. The first thing that popped into my mind was that "I done smoked some bad shit!" Again, this had me very scared. There were three of us who got out of the van smoking, but this only happened to me though and not them!

"What was happing to me," I said to myself!?

The following week was just a long week. First, I went to the local hospital and a doctor only gave me some pills and sent me home. Sometimes with MS, this happens. Without at least getting an MRI, Multiple Sclerosis is very hard to detect. If this would happen again though, I knew going out of town to get better care would be my next move. The healthcare in my hometown was just not really good in my opinion anyhow. Hopefully out of town I could find out what was going on with me once and for all. New Year's Eve while everyone else was celebrating, waiting for the countdown, I was in a daze alone. My mind was on the locking up of my body, wondering what caused it and if it was going to happen again!?

At that time the realization that they were just spasms didn't occur to me! They weren't painful, just involuntary. My face was pulled to one side and my hand just curled up. It lasted for about ten or fifteen seconds, but at the time it seemed to last longer than that. They just happened like once or twice a day at first. As the week went on, the locking up of my body started to happen more frequently than before. So that night there weren't any New Year's Eve festivities that night for me.

This night would eventually become the norm for me. After this, there would be many, many times that I would miss out on the fun and parties due to "this thing." The spasms reoccurred on the third day of the year. Running through my mind were ideas about what might be wrong with me. I had been told by friend that maybe it was a mini-stroke, but that had to be wrong because my body was locking up more than it did before. I was just hoping that it wouldn't be anything that I couldn't deal with. I mean, being admitted into the hospital and riding in an ambulance were all new to me. So, yes I was scared a little! This time my destination ended up being Pitt County Memorial Hospital in Greenville, NC where they diagnosed me with Multiple Sclerosis (MS) after a series of tests. An MRI, a spinal tap, and the scary HIV test were all done. Having these done were scary to me! The spinal tap was the most uncomfortable, but the doctor told me to be very still because too much movement could cause paralysis! After doing those tests, a man named Dr. Robert Frere came in and gave me my diagnosis. He said, "You have Multiple Sclerosis." They kept me in the hospital for four days afterward. My doctor ordered that I be given IV treatments each day, followed by some pills to treat me. By the time that I left the hospital the spasms had ceased. My doctor and I would see each other quite often over the months to come.

In the beginning physically everything felt normal, and they were. I just had to inject myself with Beta-seron(disease modifying drug) by needle every other night. Only thing was that every three months in the first year I would be admitted into the hospital to get treatment for an MS exacerbation (acute attack). The medicine was called Solu-Medrol, which was a type of Steroid treatment. At the time understanding why or how this was happenig to me was still a huge mystery. This really didn't seem fair to me. I was mad as hell, but there was no one to take it out on.

It was no one's fault! "This thing" had me so frustrated that giving up was on my mind, but I just couldn't bring myself to do it! I had come too far to give up now! To keep the people that were important to me positive, I pretended that "this-thing" was not bothering me. I like to use metaphors to explain things so I say things like," I am just taking a detour." My route to success was different, but succeeding was still my goal. Saying these things were just my cover. I was really scare as hell!

During the first year, there was this one time that I was able to drive back to Durham to visit my love, Tiffany. I had thoughts running through my mind of protecting her by not bringing my troubles into her life. The only thing that I wanted her to do was to stay focused on her studies and graduate. Tiffany bought books about Multiple Sclerosis back when I told her that I had been diagnosed with it. I just wanted things to be alright with me and her! I wondered just how much "this thing" would affect us as a team.

Then one day while at home, my first love Farrah called me. We were still okay as friends, but she found out that I had Multiple Sclerosis. She didn't really understand "this thing," and of all of her time knowing me I was so healthy. But the day that she called me, my speech was slurred, so she cried. I was talking slow and she knew that something was going on with me that I could not control, because my speech in the past was always so fast. Eventually with her studies in the health field, she learned more about MS though.

My boys and I, especially "Reese," were listening to rapper "50 Cent" a lot. At the time his music was fresh and new. It was his first mainstream album. As we listened to the album, my attitude was more like a guy who had been a "good guy" for all this time and got slapped in the face with this MS "thing." This "I don't care attitude" came out! My mind at the time was kind of rebellious. "This couldn't be right," I thought. My personality had changed a little!

There were just so many things that popped into my mind, because I was so confused. Some of the things were questions about my future. How was my life going to be!? "I had come this far trying to stay on the good side of the fence for the most part, but now I don't know!" For a long time now success had been my goal. All of the opportunities presented to me to do things that were wrong, but I chose to do what was right!? "To hell with society!" "Nice guys do finish last, I guess!?" These thoughts constantly ran through my mind. The reality of it was that my life was changing and it was out of my control! My thoughts were just all over the place.

All of this confusion caused me to slip into a state of depression. My gun was legal and although starting trouble wasn't my thing, if need be, there would be no problem for me to end it. My life seemed to have just flipped like that, but I didn't know how to change it. I was used to always having some sort of control over my life, but even that seemed to be gone now! There was just something on the inside of me telling me to separate and go in another direction from where my mind was thinking about going. Through my mind ran some crazy stuff. It felt like a game of "tug of war" was going on with my life and I was the rope. Still most of the things that everyone else did that were wrong, I didn't do. Maybe that's what caused me to be depressed?

I was a "good guy," but being this "good guy" so far hadn't seemed to pay off. The idea of coming out of close situations, bad decisions, and bad experiences had me on the fence. The way things were going in my life at that time had me furious! I didn't think the way I did as a youth anymore. The feeling of being born for greatness was still in me sometimes, but why was I feeling like it was all over!? It was like on one of my shoulders there was this angel. On the other shoulder was this devil. God was calling me, but answering Him was another thing. Thoughts of me not being worthy ran through my mind. Throughout my life things were rarely "peachy," but finishing college, according to "society," would bring an end to the lack in my life. Boy was I wrong! I just bottled up my emotions and cried as I went through this state of depression. I needed relief, but who could help me!? Holding everything in and not complaining were all that I knew to do. That really wasn't a wise thing.

Still, I wasn't a guy who was willing to go all out. I was raised to have and use my manners, to stay out of trouble, and to do my best in life. Getting into trouble was not tolerated. My grandma and my mom worked too hard for me to give up now! They still believed in me. They must have had some idea of how I was feeling inside. The thoughts that ran through my mind were both mischievous and wrong. On the low I was always mischievous with some restraint though. Maybe this was payback for that. I had deceit in my heart and on my mind. Feelings of being angry and disappointed in myself ate me up. Little did I know that my help was on its way!

# "Bottled Up Emotions"

I keep my emotions in a bottle; trying desperately not to expose them to this cold, hard world. Like soda when shaken up; filled to the top in a 20 oz. container only wanting to stay chill and gently become part of someone else. Not knowing if I am just to become waste, but knowing that I **will** quench the thirst of whoever drinks me. Please don't open my top, only to cause me to explode!? Sit me back down for awhile and try again later. Can't you tell that I'm ready to blow up in your face! Maybe you didn't take the time to look at me and see that I'm confused and getting hot wanting you to just analyze my bottle and see that my bottle contains emotions.

*--Hiekaleez--*

# Chapter Two

# Let Go & Let God

ONE AFTERNOON IN LATE AUGUST, while walking with a friend of mine from her mother-in-law's house, she sensed that lately my attitude had changed. She could tell that something had been on my mind strongly for a while. As we walked and talked, she told me that what was wrong with me sounded like depression. She mentioned this lady who could pray for me and give me some insight that would maybe calm my mind and help me get through this "state of depression" that she just figured I was going through. It had been about three weeks by that time that she noticed this. The instruction from her was to come down the street to her house before she leaves for work later that night and make the call to this lady. My friend worked at the hospital third shift, so it would be up to me to be to her house around 9:30. What I said to her was that, "I don't believe in psychics." She assured me that this person wasn't a psychic. She was a prophetess. What she could do was pass down a message from God Himself. "It wouldn't be anything bad," she said. This information went "into one ear and out of the other."

Later that night, I found myself in her living room, with no intention before of even making the call. Really, I didn't remember even walking down the street to her house. I really had no intention to go to her house. Going through my mind were the few bad things that this lady might tell me. Things that could be about my health that wouldn't be too good, my finances, or even something that had to do with a hand-gun situation. "That can't be it," I thought to myself. I just wasn't sure! They say that, "The truth hurts." Truthfully fear was the emotion that caused my hands to sweat. She called this lady who she referred to as "Sister Mckoy" upon my arrival. Later I would learn that she was the mother of a friend of mine from college. All that I had to do was to ask her to pray for me. When I got the phone all I said was, "Sister Mckoy, will you please pray for me?" She began to pray in the "natural," meaning words I could understand. Then she just started praying in "tongues," a language I didn't understand. This was my first time ever experiencing this! Then she started telling me things about myself and that "God wanted me to stay where I was and it will pay off in the long run!" "How in the world could staying here benefit me," is what I wondered!? But some of the things that she said to me about myself had to have come from God, because they never left my tongue. They were only thought by me, but never said to anyone.

The very next morning while flipping through the channels on the television at home, for some reason, the remote just stopped working when it got to the Trinity Broadcasting Network (T.B.N). Paula White was on. She grabbed my attention when she started talking about coming to God. I felt like God was really calling me then. My body just began to feel funny. Back in college there was this one time that I felt the same way, but this time was different. These people were missionaries working on behalf of God but sin was on my mind heavy back when I was in college. Well Sunday came and I was in church. It felt like being there was where I should have been the entire time anyway. It just felt so right. I was more comfortable there than in any classroom or on any football field!

Before now, going to church wasn't in my plans for the weekend at all. "I had time to get my spiritual life right," was what I always said. The next Sunday after watching TBN all of that week, I found myself in church again. Pastor Cooper gave the alter call and some force was pulling me out my seat to get up. Tears began to flow and nothing else seemed to matter to me at the time. I just surrendered. Doing things my way wasn't working, so there just had to be another way to go! The realization that the little power I thought I had, didn't really come from me. The entire time it was God! The decision to put myself up for water baptism was not a tough one for me at all. To me that was the best decision of my life!

Sunday, September 13, 2003, my walk as a Christian began. I got baptized and was saved; Hallelujah! Right away I began to serve as a Youth Minister. Sisters Artis and Johnson along with Brother Trimaine Robinson led the way. I had known Trimaine for a while, but just didn't socialize with him. Mrs. Theresa Johnson was my grandmother's friend from when they were growing up. These people that mentored me along with the youth at my church began to teach me lessons that helped me to grow as a Christian. This felt so right! I began to study from the bible that Mrs. Theresa Johnson had given me. The more I read the bible and studied, the more it began to speak to me. It was the Book of Job in *The Holy Bible* that grabbed my attention initially. Maybe it was because of how his faith remained strong even though his trials seemed so harsh? He lost so much in the beginning, but in the end everything that he lost in the beginning, he got back in the end. The phone call that my friend Kassia Day-Blanding got me to make to the prophetess spearheaded this change in my life.

"Ntyway," as my friend Tiffany would say, right away things didn't really change, but I did begin to believe in God more! My "depression" went away just like that! I understood that there was a God, and that He loved little ole me! He knew about everything both thought and done by me in my lifetime! He is the one that this life is about! It's funny how one word from Him can change your life forever! For me that was the case. After that phone call to the prophetess, I just began to just accept the fact that I had Multiple Sclerosis. After reading Montel Williams' book *Flying Higher*, what I realized was that MS doesn't have me.

This book by Pastor Rick Warren came out entitled; *The Purpose Driven Life: What on Earth am I Here For.* I studied from this book along with *The Holy Bible* and after a short while my confidence began to grow. As soon as a new year came in, I just decided to step out there and see if I could still "cut it" as an educator. The confidence in my abilities was back! Applying for a tutoring position at Halifax Community College was my first move in my quest to take back that confidence that the devil (my enemy) had stolen from me. Mrs. Iris Johnson hired me as an English/History Tutor there. I did pretty well and enjoyed every minute doing my job. My tutees commented that I was an effective tutor. Really, without them knowing it, they helped me get back the confidence that I needed to go ahead with my original plans. My dream was to teach. "This thing" had given me a little break at the time. The hospital hadn't been a trip that I had taken for some months by that time.

Leaving was tough for me to do, but it was time for me to go. The county was hiring new teachers. Over the summer I applied for a position. Mrs. Selma Allen, who was responsible for hiring new teachers, gave me a call. Back when I went to Baker's Elementary School, and she was a classroom teacher, she always had the smartest fifth graders. But by the time I got in the fifth grade, she had left the classroom. She had gotten a job at the central office of Halifax County Schools. She heard of me and my "condition," and hired me anyway. She must have "believed" in me. For that there will always be a special place in my heart and memory for her. Lots of us who got called that semester were lateral entry and need classes to become fully licensed. The county very badly needed new teachers! They were even going to pay for any classes and tests that the new teachers needed to take in order to become fully licensed. For me it would only take two courses and a test because on my transcript from college, credit had already been given to me for most of the classes that were needed. Over the summer all of the incoming teachers had to meet at the Central Office to have our New Teacher Orientation. That took ten days. Each day was hard for me! Getting the money for gas, lunch, and "this thing" (Multiple Sclerosis) tried their best to keep me discouraged. It was over the summer and that's really not the best time for me to do lots of things. Heat and MS just doesn't mix!

My teaching assignment was to a school on the other side of the county to Northwest Halifax High School. My job would be teaching U.S. History to eleventh graders. I attended Southeast Halifax High School, so Northwest was our rival back when I was in high school! Having to drive about forty miles each morning was an issue sometimes, but I was so excited and happy that it didn't even matter! The first day of school had come. I was one of the first teachers there. Nervous, but excited were just a couple of the emotions that ran through me. It was kind of how I felt just before a big game or before taking a test. It was my first time in the classroom as a teacher. "Either that day was going to be a success or I'd suck as a teacher," is what I just thought to myself!?

Anyway, while getting my classroom ready for my students to arrive, I was just grooving to some music- that I had playing-trying to get myself pumped. On the way to my office there was something in the floor that caused me to trip and fall. My cane went flying across the office and my face and neck jammed right into the closet! When I got up my entire right side was in tremendous pain! The buses with the students on them had arrived. It was a good thing that they were assembling in the gymnasium before they came into the classrooms that morning! I panicked, because my first day was just thrown its first problem, and it wasn't the students!

The staff was called to introduce ourselves to the entire student body at the assembly. The pain from the fall came just as my body was getting over an exacerbation (acute MS attack) from the summer! Really that was the last thing I needed. Not today! Not here! My dream was finally about to become a reality! Well anyway, the pain really messed up my first day experience. I thought about this book I read that my aunt had let me read one time. The title was *As a Man Thinketh* by James Allen. And I remember that my mind was on succeeding or failing the previous day and that morning too. That book was about how our thoughts and words have power, but oh well!

The way 'being in pain' was handled by me in the past was to just block everything else out. My mind went straight into "survival" mode. Just trying to make it through the day was how things had become for me, hoping each day that the next day things will be better." The only solution to my problem was to keep on going the best way that I could. My writing hand couldn't even be used to write on the chalkboard. Remembering what Harry Wong taught in those videos, I decided to delegate certain duties to my students. They loved to do things like writing the lessons on the boards and other chores anyway. We did learn to give the students certain responsibilities anyway. After all- it was their class too! It was just that I was the final authority in my classroom. With the pain, control over my classroom had been lost due to that fall. The fight had begun and I had just lost round one, metaphorically speaking. We were also taught in those "Harry Wong" videos that if you lose control of your class on the first day then it would be very hard to get it back. That little bit of warning kept going through my mind. Sooner than expected that theory would be proven wrong.

The entire first week was kind of like the first day. At the end of the first week one of my best friends Andre, was getting married on that Saturday. Just maybe after the wedding and seeing a friend of mine happy, things will change for me by then? If the new teachers would just get the sign-on bonus checks as promised to us in our orientation, then everything would be okay!? On that Friday, the secretary from the office brought around the new teachers' checks! I was so relieved. It would have been a shame if I didn't show up because of being broke! I was his "best-man." My cousin Monte rode with me because Andre was his boy too! Because I had to first, cash my check at the bank and run a few other errands, I missed the entire rehearsal. We had to drive a couple of hours there too on a Friday afternoon! So of course, traffic was kind of heavy. We did make part of the dinner though. That night the guys just hung out and the five of us

(Andre, Derek, my cousin Monte, his brother Henry, and I) just stayed to Andre's house when we went to bed. Thank God Andre didn't want to have a bachelor party! The next morning that he was to get married, we picked up our tuxedos. Man were we sharp once we got dressed! We pulled up to the wedding being chauffeured in an old Rolls Royce limousine! The rain was coming down hard! Standing beside my boy was physically tough for me but it was well worth it for "Dre". That night after the wedding- my cousin Monte and I just got a room and relaxed. That Sunday afternoon Monte ended up driving back, because we just knew that my body needed the rest. On my mind was the way things might go the next day at the school.

To me, giving up was something that I wasn't going to do! Really, I never learned how! Desperate to prove to myself that I can do this; I just went ahead to work each morning even though my mind was distracted by this pain. Some of my students recognized that "Mr. Hieke" was hurting. Some of them, of course, tried to take advantage of that by testing my intelligence. They were all intelligent, their arrogance was going to help me take back control of my classes without them even suspecting it.

An idea came to me while reading their journals and grading them one day that I didn't go to work because I wasn't feeling well. What I realized was that these students just needed someone who could relate to them. I needed to make history relevant to their lives today. I never really understood how having certain experiences in my life that didn't involve me being this "good guy" that people just assumed that I was would eventually help me out. But they would. Never judging people based on what they did or how they lived began to make sense to me. The way that I was raised along with the people that had come into my life at one point or another, actually attributed to helping me develop a teaching strategy! Understanding and being able to relate to different people would work for me. I decided to do the same thing to explain things that I always did. I loved to use metaphors to explain things.

The next morning at the school, all of the "Harry Wong techniques" that was taught to the new teachers that previous summer during the New Teacher Orientation Class was put to the side. I just had a discussion with all of my three classes when they came in. First they were told to not even open their books. We just had a heart-to-heart talk about our futures and fears. By then my pain had left me too! A colleague of mine even brought me my walking cane. She told me that she just saw it lying in the copy room. I didn't even realize that I wasn't using it! Anyway, the discussion had started with me leading off. I told them about this disease called Multiple Sclerosis first of all. Then I told them how my daily life had become living with "this thing." In our discussion about "this thing" came things that included my future and my fears. I opened the floor for a little question and answer period too. They got comfortable once they found out that there were many times that Mr. Hieke was scared just like them! Just showing them that we had a lot in common and that I do care, worked. By the end of the day we had a better understanding of each other. Once again, the classroom had become mine!

During the next four weeks of living my dream, another problem came up. One Saturday there was a "campus clean-up." My little brother came along with me to help me. The teachers had to come to get their classrooms straight, because we had people from the State Board coming to visit. We were getting a visit from the SACS Team. The school was trying to become an "accredited" school. Cleaning my classroom and moving things around caused me to get very weak. I really needed to sit! Thank God my younger brother came with me- because after my body had gotten weak- he ended up doing it himself. All I could do was supervise him on what he was to do. I was just trying to get up enough energy to drive us all the way across the county back home safely. That day my body had gotten really, really tired.

Taking control of my class back again, became somewhat "bitter sweet!" We made it back home that day, but it had become very unsafe for me to drive. Controlling my driving foot became almost impossible. It was very hard for me to move it from the brake to the gas. Out of fear of having an accident and hurting either myself or or anyone else, I made the tough decision to just sit out for a while. On my mind was my future and how not working would affect my pay for the holidays that were quickly approaching. I had feelings of just giving it up, but I didn't. I just couldn't! Mrs. Dubose-Rooks was my English teacher back in the tenth grade and she was one of the Vice-Principals at the school. She knew that just pretending to be hurt wasn't me. I just wouldn't quit easily though!

Funny thing is that being a new teacher usually you are not allowed many sick leave days with pay, so I wasn't expecting to get paid. To my surprise I was paid each month anyway! What I thought was that maybe by me being from the area and everyone pretty much knew me, someone gave me some of their sick-leave days. But no one admitted to giving me any days, so I thought nothing of it. Even though I worked very hard in rehab to get back to my work, I couldn't. I wanted to at least a little money for Christmas. December was here and it was about time for the Semester Break. There was even money in my bank account that was the exact amount of my pay, plus the Christmas bonus. I could not believe it!

This just had to be God! The prophetess was right! God wasn't done. There was more! In about a week the Spring Semester was going to start. Driving for me had gotten a little better over the break, but my confidence to drive across the county to Northwest was gone. Fear was the feeling that ran through my mind. A colleague of mine convinced me when she said during our conversation, "Fear doesn't come from God." She was a new teacher also at the same high school with me. So the next day I went ahead and drove to the school. Before I left my house I prayed to God for safety and strength. By faith, I made it there. My intent was just to inform Mrs. Arrington, who was the Principal, and Mrs. Dubose-Rooks, who was a Vice-Principal, that I wanted to return to my classroom once the Spring Semester began. We had an honest discussion in the Principal's Office about my return. After talking for a while, we concluded that it would be best if I resigned. My pride just made the decision very tough! Really it would be best for my students. I did miss most of last semester due to complications with "this thing." Returning would've just been my pride that was motivating my return. Pride like this is sinful anyway!

A good friend of mine, almost like a brother, Willie Hardy, Jr., decided to follow me home to make sure that I was safe. We had become colleagues. He saw how upset I was, so we just decided to just stop to have lunch and talk. While we ate and talked, we saw some people that we both knew, come in to have lunch also. They were being trained at the Central Office that was just down the road a l few miles. They were being trained to become "Academic Tutors." Little did I know that we would soon be colleagues. My friend Willie said that, "Everything would be okay, and it ain't over!"

After we ate our lunch I told him that, "I was okay and I could make it back home safely so don't worry about me." On the way home I just cried like a baby while listening to the radio. Thoughts of finally just giving it all up came into my mind. On the radio a guy was preaching and as he recited Proverbs Chapter 3; verses 5 and 6 the tears just kept flowing. Now only the reason for them flowing had changed. What the verses were about were trusting God. They read, "Trust in God with all of your heart, and lean not unto your own understanding. Acknowledge Him in all your ways and He will direct your paths." So that's what I meditated on all that day.

# "What Happened To All The Dreamers"

What happened to all the dreamers?
Growing up that was all I used to do!
Dream with the possibility
Of all my dreams coming true.

So many dreams, in case one should die;
On to the next dream
To work on;
At least try!

For you can't fail until you try
Is what I was told.
Not even now with my body weak,
It's never too late even when you get old.

Hold on to your dreams
Let no one take them away.
You may not believe.
But talk to God when you pray.

For He is the glue
That hold all things together
Call on Him,
No matter what people tell ya!

So never stop dreaming
That's what I said
I'll continue to dream
Until I am dead!

*--Hiekaleez--*

# Chapter Three

# God's Not Done

THE VERY NEXT MORNING I went to the local library-in Scotland Neck to research some things. While sitting to a computer with my cell phone on vibrate. Someone was calling me. It was Mrs. Selma Allen from The Central Office. She had heard about my decision to resign the previous day in my discussion with Ms. Arrington and Mrs. Dubose-Rooks at Northwest. She knew that it hurt me to do that, because I had expressed how badly my desire was to teach and to make difference in this world to her during the New Teacher Orientation. So she understood why I resigned. She called to offer me another job in education. This job would be just around the corner from my house to my old middle school. The position paid a little less, but it also required less work. The program came from a grant that was supposed to help bring the students' End of Year Test scores up in the areas of math and reading. Some students didn't score high enough to pass the test previously. I accepted the offer and went home excited and enthused once again.

Really, I wanted to be assigned to Brawley Middle School in the first place! They didn't need any History teachers at the time though. So they placed me to a high school. My idol just wouldn't retire! So that meant that they couldn't place me there yet! It felt good just to be colleagues with Mr. Johnson anyway. To hear him refer to me as, "Mr. Hieke" in front of the students made me feel very good! Just like back at Northwest High, the lunchroom during lunch was a trip that I preferred not to take. There was this one time though that I just had to go there to sit with the staff to eat. I just had to sit and have lunch with Mr. Johnson and some of my former teachers at least once! My cane aided me and even sometimes my walker, but back then it didn't even matter. Moving around had become a problem for me again around that time. I sucked it up and pushed myself to go on just a little longer. The problem with me was still my pride. Sometimes I even went to an assembly or something. I knew that I should just stop, but just stopping would feel like giving up to me.

Once again "this thing" interrupted my progress. Working at Brawley Middle School was like a dream coming true for me. When I was just beginning as a teenager in junior high school (middle school), I was "the man" there! I was the Eight Grade Class President, had top grades academically, and won many athletic awards. My plans were to try and be the coach next season, either in baseball or football, and restore athletic glory to Brawley Middle School ("Tiger-Land"). Changes were made and the progress in my students' performance was the proof! Twice a week I was traveling to Roanoke Rapids to have physical therapy after school. That was about thirty miles away from Scotland Neck. The hope was that the physical therapy that I was taking would help me, but it didn't. Frustration began to be my daily emotion at the time. Each day going to work was difficult for me. But making a difference in someone's life was my passion. How difficult things were each day for me physically, didn't even matter! There was always some student in the back of my mind expecting "Mr. Hieke" to be there each day and on time! I began to feel like just saying, "to hell with it," but my tears and my bible comforted me and kept me from just giving in.

One time Mrs. Tawana Williams, a motivational speaker, came to have a talk with the students. Actually she ended up inspiring me. She told us about how she kept pushing even though she was born with no arms. After meeting her and hearing her speak, to me there were no reasons for me to just give up. She signed her book for me. The title was *I'm Different, But I Can*. She autographed it with her feet! It was beautiful! Not long after that another test came up for me though. The message that came while reading my bible was," just stop pushing." So because of being tired of pushing and really needing treatment, I sat out again. This time it was off to the hospital once again for me. It had been a while since this happened! I was back in rehab for another visit that lasted about two weeks. By the time the hospital let me go, school was out for the summer. This time my friend Tiffany came to visit me. I honestly thought that we had a chance to be a couple after her visit.

The summer rolled on and it wasn't even on my mind to return to any school system at all. That summer I just tried my best to avoid the heat, because too much of it would mean another exacerbation (MS attack). This is a common problem for people living with "this thing." Not wanting another hospital visit, I stayed inside for the majority of the day most times. This was where you could find me. Getting hot was something that I never liked, but in the past my body could tolerate it for at least a little while. Now, when my body gets too hot I start to feel very weak and get sick to my stomach. Just imagine how my summer went that year scared to go outside, because I really didn't want to go to the hospital again! Being outside during the day on Memorial Day, the 4th of July, or even Labor Day seemed to be where people went for fun during those times of the year and I had to be inside! This made me feel like a vampire or something! My car wasn't even air conditioned! Even driving around my small town caused my body to "over-heat." The heat makes me feel miserable!

Anyway, summer was almost over and a new school year was about to begin. At this point my mom and my sister had moved in with my grandmother and me. One day a friend of mine came by my house. She had a position that needed someone in it. So she asked me to fill it. She had already heard that for me going back into the school system to work was not in my intentions at all. This job would only be for three days a week and three hours each day. She needed a G.E.D Instructor and I needed to do something! It was during the early part of the day while it was cool. So I accepted. The job was through a new grant that Halifax Community College had gotten. A site was about to be opened in my town called "Youth Link." The intent was to get those people who dropped out of school for whatever reason, get their G.E.D and a job. Halifax County did have a high drop-out and crime rate that had significantly grown at the time. First getting trained to instruct the class at the community college would be required.

The class began in October and by then I was ready. The class was a good idea! The pay wasn't a lot, but the pay wasn't a problem of mine. It was the purpose behind the entire thing. I believed in it! Just as the class began my mom moved out and I went with her. An electric power chair was given to me by Deacon Claude from my church. His father that passed away had owned it when he was alive. He really didn't want to charge me anything for it, but just to please his sister, he did. To me it didn't matter. All I wanted to do was get around a little easier. Thank God for it. Having it not only gave me back a little independence, but it was also my ride to work! I had a class, a purpose, and most importantly I had God.

This class was all part of what God was doing for me. He wanted me to see all aspects of education. From the community college, to the high school, to the junior high, and now the G.E.D class! I was lonely most of the time except for when there was either class or church. For a little while now it was as if that there was no room for me anywhere besides the class anymore. The people who were in my town that I used to be around just wrote me off it seemed at the time. Being there for my students was of the utmost importance for me. The students don't know how much the class and the students meant to me. I just had this need to be needed by someone and they were it! Anything outside of the class and church really just seemed like a former reality to me. There had to be a solution. I wanted control of my life back!

Someone told me of this lady who sold natural herbs one day while I was receiving my training at the community college to be the instructor of the G.E.D class. I gave her a call to set up a meeting with her. When my mom and I met with her she convinced me that the herbs could be the solution to my problem. The advice that she gave me was to stop taking the shot I was giving myself that my doctor had prescribed and to just rely on the herbs. At that time I was convinced that sticking myself with a needle each night couldn't have been working. I was still having acute attacks sometimes! She really was very convincing and meant well. So I took her advice! For a little while my strength seemed to be on its way back until a good friend and I were on the phone. She told me a story about someone that she knew who went to the same church that she did, who had stopped taking their doctor ordered medications. This person just began taking supplements. Soon that person's condition got worse!

What she said was always respected by me. She was about to become an attorney. Her mom **was** the woman who helped me begin my spiritual rebirth, the prophetess. Not wanting to hear what my friend was talking about though, the herbs remained part of my daily routine. I was very anxious and desperate to be healed. I thought very hard about the story that she told me. As usual she made a lot of sense to me. The herbs were just supplements. That meant that they were to be taken in addition to my doctor prescribed medication. You see the herbalist had convinced me that the medicines didn't work so I should discontinue the medicines in which my doctor had ordered me to take. In my mind they were helping me to finally improve physically. Sometimes even walking very short distances was possible for me. I said to myself, "If I'm not walking at the beginning of the year, I was going to start back with the shots my doctor ordered me to take." The beginning of the year was only about two weeks away. It had only been about a two months of not taking my prescription medication at the time!

New Year's Eve, me and my mom had gone to church to the "Watch Night Service." I couldn't believe that I stood up to give my testimony, because before now I kept my praises to myself. At the time I just used my power chair and regular wheelchair to get around. That was why I was so surprised! Once service was over weakness came back to my body. Just as my friend had told me, supplements alone couldn't heal me. My body just started feeling weaker right after church that night.

The enemy must have gotten "pissed off," because of me standing up in church to give my testimony about God and healing," is what I thought initially. Once I remembered what my friend had said to me, I just got thankful that He heard what I had told Him. But not just being patient, and letting God be God, led to me spending about twenty days in the hospital rehab. What the enemy meant for bad, my God made it good though. My stay this time would be my longest amount of time in rehab ever! Me not even returning to instruct the class was another let down. Not only was I disappointed, but so were the students that were in the class. The sad part about it was that the students had begun to believe in themselves again. With me being in the hospital, the class had to stop. That job was just for me, I guess! While in rehab this time, God had longer to deal with me and to pull me closer to Him. He really showed me some things that I could only see using my spiritual eye. There were a number of things that He dealt with me on. To get my full attention He had to separate me from lots of other people first. That's how He made sure that He had my full attention!

From January the 4th to the 24th of that year, Pitt County Memorial Hospital was where you could find me. While in the hospital lots of things took place. There was a good friend of mine named "Birdie" that passed away. My intentions had been for a long time were to get back up with him and to chill with my boy. When he passed away it was just so sudden! That really hurt me, and I cried once again! I just prayed for his family and his girlfriend, who is like my sister. Her name was Rasheida. She was one of my good friends from New York. He will always be remembered and missed by me. We became close in just a short amount of time. It was as if we had known each other for a long time though.

My birthday, which is on January 20th, was even spent in rehab. But this birthday would turn out to be one of my best ever! The staff in rehab made my birthday very special along with the number of people that were very important in my life that came by. My room was full of people! Once my room cleared and the phone to my room stopped ringing, I just sat there with the music and the television turned off and began to think to myself. Thoughts of really being loved by lots of people ran through my mind. My entire birthday was blessed and I had never even thought that my birthday would turn out like that! My "brother in Christ" Trimaine Robinson, thought that the hospital was releasing me in time for my birthday so he had planned a surprise party for me. The hospital wasn't going to release me in time for the party though. For a friend or anyone to just think of doing something like that that for me was special. He did call me earlier that day though. As I thought about how my birthday had gone that day while I was alone in my room that night I just cried as I praised God.

On the 24th of January that year I was released from the hospital, but a wheelchair came home with me. I couldn't even walk in a walker for a long distance anymore! Sometimes the remembrance of what my friend had told me about supplements pops into my mind. Stupid was how I felt. My desperation, well more like my frustration, caused me to be deceived! Isn't that something!? There hasn't been a conversation between the "Herbalist" and myself since then. She was wrong when she advised me to stop taking the medicines that my doctor prescribed, but I was the one that decided to take her advice though. She even used God's Word to fool me. To me it seemed as if "satan" had used her to deceive me. She was a very sweet lady who really wanted to help me! But what the enemy meant to harm me once again was used to by God for my good.

God revealed to me why He had allowed me to work in the field of education in the different fields that I worked in though. What the prophetess had told me had come to pass. I understood why He instructed me to stay where I was. He allowed me to briefly live **my dreams** and for that I am thankful! He had different plans for my life than I did.

Now that all of this was understood by me, it was time for me to finally just rest and trust Him (Proverbs 3:5&6), as He had told me before. After being dealt with by God for those twenty or so days in the hospital I decided to ask Him before making any huge decision in my life. So I didn't work for a while. I had to learn to wait and really trust Him. For a while at this time God was just getting me ready for the next phase. As they say, "It's all good."

# "So I Wait"

Wait patiently on the Lord
Is what it says in His Word
I just wish I had wings,
So I could fly like a bird.
No I.D., no name, but still part of God's plan.
Instead I stay grounded;
Because God made me like Adam; I'm a man!
It was because of him I was born without a clean slate.
By Jesus' death I am saved
So it's on Him that I wait!

*--Hiekaleez--*

# Chapter Four

# Things Change;
# People Change

"THINGS CHANGE AND PEOPLE CHANGE," is what a friend of mine used to say. At first I didn't really want that to be the case. It was because I didn't want to admit that she was right. It probably was because at the time, my life was seemingly not going in the direction that I thought that it should be going. While some of my friends were beginning their careers, starting their families, and/or just figuring out adult life; I was trying to just more than anything else, function with this "disability." When I got my confidence to teach I felt great! Once I got the opportunity, I still felt lonely. Being to the schools "making a difference" supposedly, was my entire motive for living. At the time I was just trying to help the students. Doing this made me feel alive and like I was doing someone else some good. That was what I always wanted to do anyway! It was what I needed as well. To me school was still all that I had, that made feel purposeful. But now even that was gone, at least for awhile! For some time now, I had been trying to work and use my hard earned degree by putting away my sinful pride. I decided to accept finances from Disability. May as well, because I did promise God that I would chill and just wait and trust Him!

There were so many questions that I still had. Questions like, what is next for me? Since, I can't teach am I still going to be successful? Is this town for me? I mean I knew that God had me, but what was He preparing me for!? Already frustrated when my friend made the statement though, "Things change, people change," I just cried that night in my room. At that time I just felt as if she really didn't care about how I felt. I just felt as if that was a weak "cop-out." It relieved her from having to even be there for me. Well, really she never "had to" in the first place. I just really wanted her there. Maybe that was my fault. The truth should have been evident to me back in college that our friendship was the same as all of her other friendships to her. When I realized that she was no respecter of persons, I understood her a little better. I didn't want anyone to feel sorry for me really, but to at least include me in their lives, especially her! I was disappointed. You see at that time God hadn't shown me the real truth yet. Later on He would. Then, I just got mad as hell with her, because of all people I just expected more than she had given me back then!

Alone and as if my past just didn't matter anymore was how I felt. I was already carrying this load the best way that I knew how. It didn't erase the fact that I was scared and wanted my friend. At that time my mindset had gotten a little better I thought! But what do I do next!? In my mind I knew that I was going to get back control of my life with or without her. Once I accomplished this, she'd see. My last time in rehab, I sat up one time lunging for her to get me a hug, and it was only a dream. See, for some reason her not being around me at all, just hurt! I was going through physical changes with my body that I didn't understand. Along with that my social life was quickly changing!? I was just so very frustrated. Inside I knew that these changes had to take place in some form, but I never thought that the day would come that she and I didn't talk. Truthfully, certain "friends" and I were growing further and further.

Before having that experience of her standing at the end of my hospital bed, I sent her a long angry email. My intent was to just hurt her with my words. The very next morning she was to the end of my hospital bed! I got so excited. Then I realized that I was only dreaming that she was there. I looked up at the television and it was on Pastor Corbitt from Community Christian Church in Greenville, NC was talking about how our friends are only people. They are not God! He talked about how God is our "real friend" and how putting a lot of focus on our "Earthly" friendships without Him, was just like worshipping false idols. No relationship is supposed to be put before our relationship with God. Realizing what I had done, I just prayed to God to just fix me. I was literally crying in my bed and I could feel me getting lighter. And as the tears that rolled down my face stopped, I started to feel lighter and lighter! Something else was changing. I wished that there was a way to take back all of that bad stuff that I said. Thank God that she understood and didn't hold it against me.

The reality of it was that things and people must change though. The guys that I used to always be around from my hometown just did their thing, but I was pursuing something else. I had to really "man up!" God had given me different directions. I knew that some things just had to change in my life, but I really didn't want them to! My other guys, the ones that I played ball with and went to college with, just stepped up for me in a way that was really unexpected. Our friendships grew tighter and when I saw them, my eyes lit up like a Christmas tree and I just thanked God for them. At that time I needed some Earthly friendships in my life; some positive ones that reminded me that if I needed their support I had it. My other "brothers" "Koodie,"Andre, and T.R had moved away to different states. So my other boys' support was just enough for me and I didn't get hooked. They had careers also, but they had time to include ole "Hieke." They just were trying to keep me mindful that it wasn't over and that to them I mattered. Even a "muscle man" needs someone to "spot" him at times. Our coach did say that later in life that we would see the game of football was like life. "No matter how tough it gets, you just have to keep going." For me at the time that he said that I really didn't pay him any mind. Football was just something that kept me around people, allowed me to hit people legally, and that people said I was good at!? Most of the friends that helped me maintain a positive life outlook were the guys that I went to war with on the gridiron though. So coach was right after all!

I believe around that time I had started to isolate myself from a lot of people though. This came after life began to change for me. The fact that my life would never be the same hit me like a sack of bricks. In the past being around the masses didn't bother me. Because of the visits to the hospital at the onset of "this thing," the confidence that had taken a while for me to build up was gone. People seemed to just write me off because Multiple Sclerosis was still so mysterious of a disease. Some really didn't know how to deal with it, but **hell,** I wasn't asking them to have "MS" for me or anything! All I really wanted was their companionship. Realistically the isolation was probably what was needed. I wanted people around me, but I ended up finding myself being alone most of the time. I hated it! Man, was it hard! Things were about to change some more for me though.

My independence, goals, and my life plans seemed very "blurry." Well at that time, God seemed to have left me to figure things out on my own. So people that I counted on to be there for me had gone, my body was not doing what my mind was telling it to do, and it seemed as if God had bounced on me. Thoughts like, "Man I give up the other way for Your way and You leave me hanging," ran through my mind!? But knowing that this had to happen and that He is always there, kept me on track. I had to get past it because without me knowing it, the future held this harsh reality in store for me. God had me in "detox" from this world. Kind of like they do in a drug rehab program, I suffered from "withdrawal." There were good days and bad days. It was on the bad days though that my mind brought the memories back of my former years (life). That wasn't enough to win back my soul though. "This thing" has to do better than that! He did tell me that,"The best is yet to come," so I could just relax.

I just remembered what the prophetess did tell me about God was just testing me and so that made it all good. To be chastised by God makes the silence bearable. If you think about it, during a test the teacher is quiet though. The more I think about it God must have had great plans for me huh!? Still though this "new reality thingy" was not easy at all!

I was able get some things in my personal life right that needed to be taken care of. It had gotten to the point, when I was living with my mom, that a home aide would be needed for me. This aide would be responsible for helping me to get bathed, dressed, and fed each day. At first I really didn't want any help other than my mom, grandma, or maybe my uncle. I had a talk with my cousin Cassandra and we were talking about our big cousin and how she was actually overqualified to be my aide, but she accepted the job. Putting my pride aside, I realized that this was a great decision! She was the perfect person to help me too! Her name was Kejak. We grew close and eventually my relationship with my entire paternal side got better. It was not bad, but it was just the way that my dad handled not being in my life growing up that kind of screwed everything up. Honestly speaking, our relationship got better when I was officially a grown man and that was the problem. But really, I always just wanted them to accept me. Just before my grandfather Haywood Alston passed away, I believe we really began to grow close. Well really before that, my relationships with my dad, my siblings through him, and some of my cousins had gotten better. Someone had to tell me stories about our grandfather.

As far as I could remember my dad's last name was Draughn and to me that was my family, so I had always been okay. Shoot, they helped to raise me! They helped to make my Christmas each year joyous. It was him who took me to get my first haircut. In my eyes he was my dad. Anyway God knows what's best for us all and at that time, the Draugh family was best for me. For a while now I had grown distant from the Draughn family, but when I went to college my grandma bought me some things that I would need anyway. At graduation one of my aunts, from the Draughn family, was there. And when I was in the hospital, they came too. So yeah, I was loved greatly! God made sure that I never went unloved during my stay here on Earth.

What God was doing it seemed; was fixing my family situation. Already He made it so that I ended up living with my mom and at the same time fixing it with my paternal side. Each day seemed to be routine. I woke up early. My cousin/aide came over to help me. Really I expected her to come and I needed somebody to talk to each day as well. For a while now it had only been she and God that I talked to regularly. There were a few visitors to come to check me out though. It was never the guys in town that I used to roll with though, of course. Well besides my cousin Monte, my boys Earl Mills, Jr. ("E.J."), and Trimaine, came by every now and then. God was just showing me who was who. Alot of the guys that I played football with me back in high school and graduated with me talked to me a majority of the time. These guys who visited me and kept check on my mental welfare. It would later be those guys who were my main "click."

There were instances that some of the same guys came over to my house in Scotland Neck. We had a small cookout with just us sometimes. The guys were mainly from Enfield, and by me living in Scotland Neck, they weren't too comfortable around the town. I would like to think that those people with some of them silly "town rivalry" mentalities have matured anyway. See, I never really had it and my boys really weren't a target. In the past that might not have mattered though. Sometimes somebody from over there picked me up too. I must have been considered to be brave, but to me I wasn't, because we were all men by then. I am a grown ass, working man, who paid my taxes to go anywhere I please in America! Having family members who were respected in Enfield helped too!

Things were about to change some changes that happened, I didn't even know it. Sometimes I just felt like throwing in the towel. But there was just this thought in my head about giving up! Well, by then I was a believer headed for Heaven, but I just wish that God could give me a "cheat sheet" or something!! What's next for me now!?

# "I Lunged For You and You Pulled Away"

What's going on?
I needed you the other day!
So close, yet so far;
I lunged for you and you pulled away.

Was it something I said?
Maybe something "I" done?
I mean could it have been that bad;
That you'd want me gone?

I thought that you cared.
Maybe that was back in the day;
Because today I needed you.
I lunged for you and you pulled away.

I mean don't you see me
The way that I see you?
I always looked at you like blood
But you ran and didn't help me through.

Remember, when you lunge for me,
I'll break your fall; I won't stray.
You lunge for me and I PROMISE
Not to pull away!!!

*--Hiekaleez--*

# Chapter Five

# Starting Over

MY BROTHER WAS AWAY TO a group home because somewhere in between my second and third visit to the hospital, he began to have issues himself. It had gotten to the point that it had become just too unsafe for him to remain in the home. Things became very unsafe and difficult with him in the house! My mom had to place my little brother in a group home. He needed help. My mom couldn't provide the kind of help he needed. Protecting my family and providing for them was all I ever wanted to do. But brother was going through something that I couldn't help him with. Every now and then he had these episodes where he would hear a voice telling him to kill himself. This was serious! I believe that it was the taking of all of the different medicines that these "mental health" doctors prescribed to cover their inability to adequately diagnose my brother.

The doctors first said that he was hyper-active and that he was AD-HD. Then they tested him for being Autistic. Then it was for being Bi-Polar. There was just this feeling that my little brother needed help and that help couldn't come from me! He began to do well at this group home-except for a few incidences he had while there. These incidences caused him to be placed in mental hospitals. When my brother used to begin to have these psychotic episodes were the only times he would have to be placed in the hospital. To me the damage had already been done when the doctors were just "guessing" when he was just a small boy. What I saw was a sweet kid with many gifts but he just had no push. He had dreams. The problem began mainly, when he began to relax with the idea that he was what they said he was. You see kids used to tease him, because he was different. The schools even allowed this when they labeled him AD-HD. It seemed that once he found out that he was "special" he began to act the way "they say" that he should. Well, we all are "special," but he used the fact that they called him "special" in a not so good way.

It began to feel as though we just had to move-to start over! The place that I had always called "home" began to feel like a totally different place to me now anyway. In Scotland Neck, I felt invisible and as if I was in a strange land or something anyway. My agenda was to leave before I lost my mind. One day my mom came to me and she told me that she was thinking about moving. "She must have read my mind," I thought to myself! A smile came on my face. I said to her, "Me too!" The place that she was talking about was perfect. Greenville! Moving to Greenville really made sense. A change of scenery was in order for us. People didn't visit me much anyway, we went there often to see my brother, and the schools there were better for my sister.

Greenville, North Carolina seemed to be where we came a lot. The group home that my brother lived in and the hospital that I was in a lot, were there. My neurologist also was in Greenville. The name of his office was East Carolina Neurology. Greenville really did know MS. In July of 2006 we moved to Greenville. It was hot and humid the day that we moved. With this "MS" that wasn't a good thing. I was able to do more than before there. I felt free to "reinvent" myself. For some reason I just felt different.

The neighborhood that we moved into was perfect for me. The apartment was handicapped accessible and everything! There was more than enough room for me to navigate through the apartment in my wheelchair and all. Going into my closet, going outside, and to the bathroom on my own were all possible in this apartment. It was affordable and all! My doctor's office was practically right across the street now. Moving there was really a great idea, but the only thing was that I still felt lonely! At least the reason I felt that way was that the area was new to me. Back in Scotland Neck I was in the town where my "friends" were, but hardly anyone visited me so "what the hell!" So really not having visitors didn't bother me anymore. This is where I needed to be. When we first moved there, we didn't know many people. Staying home and going to church somewhere were mainly my activities. My sister and my mom met new people, but I just kept to myself. People probably thought that I was crazy or something, because when I sat outside all I used to do was smile and sit. I was just mainly observing different people and their personalities. There were many other resources that could help me in Greenville. Over time I would learn what they were.

Being there allowed me to think a lot and to be clearer about my identity. In the first year in this new city, I did patch up a relationship that was really important to me. My girl Stephanie did understand me a little better. She empathized with me. I believe her mother had a talk with her and she realized that it wasn't her. I just was having a difficult time dealing with being in the state that I found myself. My life just flipped on me and for what!? Still for a while not being able to do lots of things affected me. Because there were lots to do, but finding out how they could be done was up to me. Things that most people took for granted were the things that I dreamed about being able to do. If only I could walk and stand lots of my issues probably wouldn't even exist! Not walking took away my independence!

While reading the *Bible* I came across Job 3:25. It read, "For the thing that I greatly feared has come upon me, and what I dreaded has happened to me." For me it seemed as if He (God) was talking to me. I've always feared depending on others. Someone's help to get out of bed, to get dressed, and to even prepare my meals sometimes were needed. It would be a perfect stranger that helped me. This time it wouldn't be a family member. There were times that this fact caused me to just want to scream! These "aides" didn't seem to be trained. It probably was because before moving, my aide was so good. She must have spoiled me. No, even though my aide was my cousin back in Scotland Neck, she was completely professional first. In the first nine months of living in Greenville I must've had about five different nurse's aides. And needing their help was already a big adjustment for me.

It had to have been a little over four years with this disease. But by then, it had been about a year and a half year at that time I couldn't walk at all. "My independence was gone and because of that, a stranger has to see me naked and clean my butt," is how I used to think. Now I understand that sometimes God allows things to happen in our lives that sometimes don't really understand the reason why. Immediately my mind reverted back to what was told to me before we moved to Greenville. One night the prophetess once again prayed (prophesied) for me. She told me that, "The best is yet to come" and "Right now you are just being tested," for the second time. At the time figuring out what would be on the test was still a mystery to me. They say that the help was in the *Bible,* but for some reason the answers hadn't hit me yet.

As time rolled on new people that crossed my path. Most of them were there to help me, but of course there were a few people who either took advantage of my situation or at least tried. For instance there was this one guy who came to me all friendly and since I didn't have many buddies in Greenville yet, but I thought that maybe we could become good friends. He messed that up when he betrayed me by stealing from me! The fact that it was from my home that he stole from me, only intensified the act. He told me that he was from New Orleans, Louisiana and used the devastating Hurricane Katrina as his excuse for even being in Greenville, North Carolina. According to him that as a result of the hurricane he and his family were forced to move as were many of the victims. For a while he used to cut my hair and actually he did a great job! He told me that before Katrina hit, cutting hair was what he did professionally.

One day it was raining and he couldn't cut my hair outside. For some reason my mom had left the house. Since it was about his the fifth time of cutting my hair and by just talking to him on my porch, I invited him to just come inside of the apartment to "trim me up." Boy, was that a mistake! He somehow stole from me in my home! What he stole from me is kind embarrassing to talk about, but I just may as well tell it all. He had a 38 caliber pistol and needed bullets for it. My pistol was of the same caliber. I offered to give him a few of mine, since I thought that he was really a "friend" of mine. I pulled out my gun gave him some because my clip was full and I had extras. Mine was a .38 caliber Highpoint- pistol. Showing him my gun turned out to be a big mistake. When he left, I realized that he taken my gun! My guards usually stayed up when I first met people. I should have never taken my eyes off of him. Thank God for Jesus, because he could have really hurt me! Why in the world did I let him in so quickly is a mystery to me!? You would think that I knew better. Back in college, my guards were always up. Durham was known for being violent and people really would stab you in the back. That's where my school was located. There a person's word and their actions sometimes didn't match each other. Getting over on me hasn't always been so easy in the past so why now!?

Having "this thing" must have something to with it!? Nah, I won't blame my condition for everything. I was just plain ole sympathetic to his unfortunate situation and stupid! Being sympathetic was just me! Making excuses was something that I never really liked to do, but found myself doing it too much back then. By my gun being legal and registered, the police were called and I did file a report. Anyway I prayed for him still, because I later learned that he had a drug addiction and that he lied to me. The only truths that he told me were that his mom had cancer and that he was a dad. Praying for him and his family was all I could do about that. My "street smarts" were back and so were my guards. They instantly went back up!

When I moved to this new city, my doctor ordered therapy to take place right in my home. This was very convenient! After having therapy for a couple of months, I was able to walk with the aide of my walker about thirty feet. That was the distance from my back room to the front door. This excited me! This was short-lived. Medicaid Insurance would no longer cover the cost of me getting therapy at home being that I was able to get out and go to a therapy facility. In the home the therapists were limited anyway, because they had more resources at their facility. So I understood. Transportation was needed and they told me about transportation that I was eligible for. I did receive Medicaid Insurance in the past.

Soon therapy at the Day Rehab facility that was next to the hospital began for me. There they focused on three disciplines, Recreational, Occupational, and Physical Therapies. It was the things learned during the recreational therapy time that I used the most and soon. I was made aware of the different resources that could hopefully help me gain more of my independence. Going away from my home going to the library the Pitt Area Transit System (P.A.T.S), gave me back some of my independence! Once I found a barbershop to frequent, transportation took me there also. It had been a while since I even went inside a barbershop! The wait time was long, but with "this thing" it was advantageous for me to become more patient and communicate with other people anyway. Over time God gave me those qualities. So they help me in my efforts to adapt to my new environment. Going to the library and the barbershop just made me feel "alive" again. For a long time now, I hardly dealt with people. At these places, my disability seemed to not matter! All I been wanting to do was to feel like I "belonged" again!

My sister started a new school that she adjusted to well. As expected, she did well in her schoolwork as well as with making new friends in our building. Some of her new friends were even in our neighborhood. She kind of reminded me of myself. My mom, my sister, and I seemed to be doing okay. We still hadn't found a place to attend church regularly yet. Pastor Cooper from back home knew this deacon who lived in Greenville and referred us to his church. The name of the church was Philippi Church of Christ. The pastor there was Pastor Randy Royal. It just so happened that I remembered him from when we were in rehab together at the hospital in worship. He was there as a result of a severe stroke that he suffered. I didn't know that he was a pastor though. I did think that he was a deacon or something. After all of this time, he still remembered me though. This was my first time attending a big church. This church had services at 8 a.m. and at 11 a.m. on Sundays! The church from which we come from was small. This church just didn't feel like the right one for me to commit myself to! It seemed like just a larger Shiloh from which we had come. There just was something that my soul was searching for and it just wasn't here. The congregation was just like the one I left, older and predictable. Things just didn't feel different. It felt as though there was a script that the people followed and sometimes it just didn't feel like most people there really radically had the faith that I sought. The church seemed to be stuck in their ways. It didn't feel like there was room for me to grow there or places to use my God given gifts. I wanted and needed a place that was about change, but always about God!

When my birthday came later in January of the next year some of my boys came to celebrate with me. It was Hardy, Debro, the twins (Shuntee and Duntee Silver), my cousins Monte and his son Mondre that all were in the house. Kacee Hardy came too, who eventually became Kacee Hieke after she married my cousin Monte. We had a great time as usual. I needed that from those guys. Other people gave me some phone calls. Over all my birthday was wonderful again!

Well anyway during my hunt for the right place to worship, I gave Independent Living a phone call. This was another great resource that was available to me here in Greenville. There they assigned me to a Recreational Therapist. Her name was Deshayna. Her goal was to get me involved in doing things and just to enjoy my life in general. It was the day that I accepted her invitation to attend an Adaptive Sports Day event at East Carolina University that helped to change my mentality a little. There were people with different disabilities who were active there. They shared their stories with me. Some of them had never before or never will have some of the great experiences that I've had in life. They were still just so beautiful in attitude. They made me realize just how blessed I really was! It was at that moment that the reality of me not being able to complain just hit me "like a brick!" Some never walked before let alone play sports and drive. After seeing them and hearing their stories, I felt like my situation was nothing and that I owed it to them to become a voice for or with many of them. Really I just thanked God for all of His blessings bestowed upon me. How dare I complain!?

Months later the Recreational Therapist invited me to a beach retreat with some of her clients for the weekend. I went then too! It was just something about the spirits that most of the others with disabilities had. At the camp fire one night Ms. Jaylee and I, at the time, were sitting beside each other and just talking as the entire camp ate some "smores" and talked. I only call her by her first name because "a little birdie" told me that she has gotten married since then. We talked about writing a book. She was very smart and was already in the process of writing one herself. She was awesome and her spirit that weekend really had an impact on me. Mr. Murray whom I met on day one, immediately took on the responsibility of helping me get around the entire weekend. That was so special to me. For that I'll never forget him! Getting out and doing things with people that had different kinds of limitations also, whether it was physical or mental, helped to change my mentality drastically. Being ashamed to be me had been buried. My life may have changed, but it was no where near to being over! The devil is a LIAR!

After coming to stay home with us on weekends and my mom being called to do many things that the Group Home did for my brother before we moved to Greenville anyway, after Christmas Break she decided that he may as well stay home with us. Each day my mom had to take him to school. But she already did this when he was living in the Group Home anyway. I decided to diagnose his condition myself, as the "Peter Pan syndrome." He is getting older, but in the mind he never wants to grow up. Anyway his mentality hadn't changed. In that Group Home it seemed like he was only being baby-sat there and that's it. They did nothing else for the guys there it seemed. There was no after school help with homework, no group seminars, no kind of physical recreation time or anything. Oh, the way that they handled situations that came up with these boys was to send them home or commit them to a mental hospital. There were times that my brother was made upset by someone else in the home. He had an episode and they sent him away. He wasn't hearing the voices anymore though, but he still had serious issues socially. I kind of felt sorry for the guy but sometimes he made me tired of him and his issues to be honest. Psychologically they were impacting us all. It was like we were always walking on egg shells in my own home. My problem was not that he had his issues. He never tried to use the techniques that his therapist worked with him on. We both had issues, but I believe it was the fact that he just never used the techniques that he had been taught that bothered me.

Before he came into the house with us, my mom and I were trying to live a godly life. My mother was studying her Bible more and she was becoming a woman led by faith and all. She was not smoking as much, almost none. And I had almost stopped with the smoking of my little cigars. But trying to stop doing these ugly things wasn't easy for either of us, being that he stressed us out. I don't believe he ever understood this!? Well I guess that was more of an excuse. There is no excuse for sin though. The house was peaceful most of the week and all.

My mom continued to take on different odd jobs that the temp service came up with, but just not the right one. She took this third shift job. This job showed promise to be "the one." After working on this job for a while it seemed as if she was going to be made permanent. My mom got 'the bright idea' to move. Then it sounded like an okay idea, but out of frustration and lack of patience to just wait on God, it wasn't so good of a decision after-all. This move began to take away my freedom. You see she wanted to get an apartment that had three bedrooms to accommodate the growth in family size in the home. This apartment was a little more expensive and in a quieter neighborhood. It was closer to the hospital, but for me it was just a little too quiet! There I would need more help going in and outside, it was tougher to get in the bathroom for me, and my closet was smaller. Before, my wheelchair could get in the entire bathroom. My boys Harrison and Willie helped us with our move, but my mom told me when she went to check the apartment out that the accessibility was right for me and all.

Around that time, I had been to numerous seminars that were being held about this new "wonder drug" for Multiple Sclerosis that was named Tysabri. Before I even left Scotland Neck and moved to Greenville, there was a "recall" placed on the treatment. Someone had died after receiving a treatment. My doctor just thought that if I took the Solu-Medrol, the steroid treatment, too long then I might get Diabetes. He didn't want me to get another chronic disease trying to treat my "MS." It had been about a year since it had been off the market being tested. They wanted to see just what caused the unfortunate death of this gentleman. People were just so reluctant to take this drug once it was back on the market, that the MS Society held seminars about it, to ease people's fears. After attending these seminars and reading up on it for myself. I just prayed and decided to give it a try. I trusted my doctor and all, but I just trusted God more! When I thought about it, at least each night I would no longer have to give myself a shot if I took this!

Anyway, moving to this new place wasn't such a good idea after-all. I thought that it would be at first, being that my mom knew of my situation and needs. She once again assured me that the move there would be good for all of us. Really where we already lived was okay with me! I lacked the courage to speak up though. She wasn't happy with where we were already and to me, like always, my goal was to make my momma happy. See before, she and my sister shared a really large room and I had my own room in an apartment that was designed for a "disabled" person. Now that apartment really wasn't designed for me. Things were supposedly about to get better, but they didn't! Things seemed to be going in reverse. There was no community in that neighborhood. It was very boring. Over time I would begin to feel very limited again! We didn't receive a lot of help. We had to pay bills, get food, and all off of very little funds. All we had were two SSI checks coming in, her job as a "temp", and no food stamps. We had to watch every dollar hard! I just knew, by mom always catching on so fast at a job, that when she tests to be permanent again; she'd pass and then maybe things would change.

Well my mom scored high, but I guess it wasn't enough to qualify for permanent. After a while her "temp" hours were gone and she had no job. So, we could no longer afford the apartment. Then one morning there was this preacher on television. I could swear she was talking to me when she preached. Boy had it been a while since this happened to me! Right away, I liked her. The church had a 'Family and Friends' Fun Day and on the telecast she was inviting everyone to just come out and fellowship with them. We went to this event that Saturday. I had to see what this church was about. The name of the church was Koinonia Christian Center Church. It meant "Authentic Fellowship" and I could tell just how genuine and inviting these "church folk" were when I first visited. My mom lost her temp job because her hours had run out and she wasn't made permanent, but on my mind was my worship. I needed answers and God had them all! I just felt like it was through this lady on television, that He would give them to me.

That Sunday my family attended church there. Attending church there helped me to finalize my decision to make this church my home. I had found a church finally! When the pastor did the alter call, she said tha+t if it was anyone's first time attending services there she didn't want us to join, but I was already sold after being there that Saturday. The fact that we had to wait until the second visit there to join had me so anxious that entire week! So the next Sunday, I just couldn't wait until she did the alter call at the end of her sermon. Once she did though, we answered! I just had to become a member there. There was a short wait time before a New Membership Class would be offered. Taking the class was required before we would become official members. Coincidentally when we moved again, the place that we moved to this time was about one mile from the church.

# "Are The Eyes Soul's Window!?"

When you look through my eyes
Tell me just what do you see!?
Can you see that I'm hurting!?
That normal is what I want to be!?

Can you see that I miss walking?
Can you see me getting up from that serious blow?
You can't see what I hide
Because I don't want you to know

Cause I'm afraid to show
Scared of what you might do
You might run from me
Instead of helping me through

Do my eyes tell you that!?
Tell me. Can you see!?
I'm a caged Eagle
Wanting to be set free

My eyes should tell you that I am a child of God
Chosen to make an impact on at least a few
And a change in those that want to fly
The way that I once flew

Before that serious attack
On my strength and my soul
So tell me did see all of that
From my soul's window!?

*--Hiekaleez--*

# Chapter Six

# A Place to Call Home

As soon as we moved we received a letter in the mail to begin our class for 'New Members Orientation' at K.C.C. The class took only a few hours on a Friday evening and early on Saturday morning. It didn't really matter; this was now officially the home that I was looking for. The pastor was dynamic and so was everything else I was looking for in a church. I enjoyed the Word, the love, the choir the room for growth and all! This was just the right place for me and I was excited! Right away God began speaking to my spirit through her, Pastor Rosie S Oneal. There were even ministries for the young. I was proud to say that I was a 'Koinonia Man'!

In the beginning after Bible Study there was a group that we met with every other week. My pastors there set up this 'family small group' idea so that we could discuss certain topics. Because there were thousands of people who were members there, the groups were designed to provide more intimate support. I thought that the groups meeting after Bible Study was a great idea. At first we made it to everything. We didn't miss church, bible study, or our groups. We signed up for and joined our specific group. My mom and I joined certain ministries and all. It felt great being so involved with what was happening at the church. The church was recognized as a "Mega Church" in Greenville. The church was popular. Our senior pastor was officially confirmed as Bishop Rosie S. Oneal! She wasn't just our pastor but was a pastor of pastors. To us she was already a bishop. We already referred to her as "Bishop" sometimes. There was a Koinonia in Youngsville, NC, one in Virginia, and there was even Koinonia in Africa. You see this was what I was talking about! A church that was on the move, growing! Growth was what not only what I needed, but it was what I wanted.

When the church first began there were only seven members, but now she was pastor to thousands. It must have been the style that she used to preach and just the personality of the church altogether that grabbed my interest. Bishop liked to use metaphors when she taught. I said taught because when she preached it was more like she was teaching. Just like the church members our pastor was mixed in ethnicity. The church wasn't identified by any certain denomination. There, the only thing that identified the church was that it was truly about God. It didn't matter how much money you had, how you looked, or where you came from. Now some people who didn't really know this for themselves assumed that it was like a lot of churches, based on the material things. But I once had this teacher back in the sixth grade that told us what the word "assume" meant which I thought was funny but true. It was Mr. James Wesley, who was a very smart man and had a strong impact on my life, who did that. He said that, "When you assume you make an **A**SS out of **U** and not **ME**." The church was not at all like that.

The pastor herself gave more money than most people I knew of personally anyway. She was very down to earth and that made me really feel comfortable. She prayed diligently for us all. There were many things that the church did and not just around Greenville, but around the world. There was room in the many ministries at the church to serve. At the time I wanted to serve in so many ministries, but "this thing" kind slowed my start. Well me being me, I wanted to be more involved right away, but I just decided that first I'd get familiar with the church. As time went on, I grew more spiritually and got more familiar with the church, but of course my progress was slowed even more, because my involvement there hit a rough patch.

My mom later landed a great job. Since we moved to Greenville she wanted this. She did have to work and she always worked hard when she had a job. She worked so well that she was given lots of hours to work. When she got the job we began missing church and the bible study nights. I still wanted to attend regularly. From my wheelchair I had a very hard time getting there, even though it was only about a mile from where we moved. Man was I getting frustrated! I couldn't believe that. Sometimes I guess being in a "mega" church some people get looked over. The problem was me mainly. My inability to just go when I wanted to had gotten me just a little frustrated at this point. What I realized though one day was that there was no handicapped accessible buses at this church. When I joined I noticed the church buses, but never noticed that there were no buses for people that were in a wheelchair as I was! This wasn't right because people with physical disabilities need and love God too!

At the time it seemed as if everyone owned a sport utility vehicle (S.U.V) and getting into one of those things at the time for me was very difficult. The way that I did when I did go with my mom, was wheelchair to car transfers. When it was hot outside you have to figure how hot a car was to my hand when I transferred into one. When it rained, the transfers were very difficult too. The fact that I am heavy didn't help either! Some days I felt too weak to transfer period. When I went to the barbershop or library I did use the transit system that was an accessible van. The fact that church had no handicap accessible van, once my mom pulled back because of work, affected my spiritual growth even more.

I had to do something, but "What will I do!?" Being seriously involved is what I wanted very badly!

Sometimes I can't talk to her physically, by her being on the go a lot, I wrote her a letter. In those letters, I told her things like how I am doing, what I'm believing God to do in and for me, and just sometimes writing to let her know how a great a pastor I think she is and all! As busy as she was she always took a little time from her hectic schedule to write me back. So in one letter to her I expressed the need for a handicapped accessible van. One day in church she mentioned that the church would be trying to acquire one. That was like music to my ears. With one of those in place, I could be just as involved as the next man! By now being ashamed of going out in my chair had diminished. But I was tired of being discriminated against, especially since all that I wanted to do was experience God like everyone else! That's the way my pastor is. Just tell her your problems and if she can, she will try to fix it. See before the need for one hadn't been expressed to her. Since I did that and she knew that my letter was for real, she obliged. In the meantime as we waited for God to bless the church with the means to get one I just kept going whenever I could!

My pastor had 'World Missions' in her heart and on her mind. God gave this to her. I mean our church's theme for the year was "Blessed to be a blessing." Later she and some other church members took a trip to Belize, South America to spread some Christian love over there. They filmed the entire trip. At the service after their return someone who went with her showed a clip of their visit in church. It was right then that our pastor made the announcement that she realized that there were people right here at home hurting. So she decided to give a home to someone and to give someone money to catch up on whatever bills they were behind on. See during the recession, lots of people were losing their jobs, homes, savings, and other things. To even attain one of these two gifts you had to do an application first. I wondered what happened to the accessible vehicle though. I mean all of that was very important at the time. I didn't want to sound selfish, but all I wanted was to serve God! I needed to be more involved! But if God told her to do that first then who am I to disagree!? After giving out the help to people in need, it was time for some of my prayers to be answered.

One day she announced that the church was still going to purchase an accessible van for the people who needed to ride it. There were thousands of members, but I only knew a few. Most of the time, some of the members might have thought that my mom was my wife. We were together most of the time that we came to the church! I felt that this was the reason most of the attractive women there never said anything to me. Really, once we get the van, I just knew that this would change. Just like when I went to college, the females weren't my reason for being there, but it didn't hurt at all that they were there and that they were attractive to my eye! My passion and purpose was mainly to serve God!

I could go to the church without my mom once the church got the accessible van. It would maybe even give me the opportunity to mingle a little more as the single man that I was. Sometimes I wanted to be to the church and my mom may have been too tired or just didn't feel like it. I wasn't just going to church, I was "God hunting." I wanted all that He had for me. Finding me a female friend to hang out with would only be a bonus! I maybe could find my wife there. *The Bible* does say in Proverbs 18:22 that, "he who finds a wife finds a good thing, and finds favor from the Lord. So, very soon the church just had to get a ride that was accessible!

# "Invisible"

Do I have powers that no one told me about!? Is my normal voice so low that I have to shout!? If it is tears you are looking for then I'm just sorry because it is tears that you won't see. I cry when I'm alone; just God and me. You see, I can trust him not to tell, because He already knows! No matter where or what I go through He always goes.

I cry because I see people even though people tend not to see me. It's okay because I'm just a diamond that's being polished and one day when people realize my shine they'll all want to see! I don't desire to be famous, I just know my worth. My price was decided the night that a girl named Mary gave birth. When her son named Jesus gave His life for me, He decided my cost. He made a way for me to live forever with Him. He came back and is always here to rescue the lost.

So when you walk past me don't look at me and stare. You have no idea of my pain, entire story, or despair. If you make it to Heaven, just look me up and one day I'll be there! Oh, that's right you didn't get to know my name! Could it be possible that you didn't recognize me from before because to you I seemed invisible!?

Never look past a man and assume to know his worth. Priceless may be his value. You'd know that if you sought God first.

*--Hiekaleez--*

# Chapter Seven

# **Stuck**

THIS TIME I REALLY DIDN'T care too much for this place either. It wasn't handicap accessible and there really wasn't much room for my wheelchair! This place wasn't comfortable at all for me. Moving there was a desperate move for us. The things that I could do were very limited. This time the apartment was even more inaccessible for me than the last place! Sometimes it just felt as if I was living in a bad dream or something! My mom told me that this was only a temporary place. It was just until she got a better job. Because when we first moved there she hadn't gotten that job yet. Feeling guilty for being a "special needs" person, I thought that just maybe my family would give me more help if I helped them out more financially. That was so far from the truth!

It was killing me that at the time my finances were very limited. Really I needed more help because of the way that the apartment was set up. It was impossible for me to even get into the bathroom there at all! In the last place at least getting into the bathroom was possible, but just barely! Neither of the last two places were like the first apartment though. Then, my health really had started to improve. Once again I needed help to get into and out of my home.

"I am just so tired of my life being like this," is what I said to myself.

Even something so simple as being able to take a shower was gone. By that time, it had been gone for about two years! It seemed like since my brother came to live with us, my living condition had worsened. It had gotten to the point that it seemed as if all that was left for me was hope! Hoping that my health was restored and that I moved somewhere that was more accessible for me were what I just craved! All that I could think do, was to just keep praying and meditating on God's promises to me. Our new church home being about a mile from us now was a plus though!

Maybe I could find refuge there!?

The church took a serious interest in my new neighborhood. It had to have been because that neighborhood had a reputation of being overly violent because of the gang situation. In the past the neighborhood had gotten terrible as a result. Before Hurricane Floyd back in 1999 neighbors say that it was a better neighborhood. Afterward though, the people that moved to that area just brought the neighborhood down. Being there brought on other troubles that didn't really involve me. It was filled with people who seemed to have no serious goals in life. They seemed to be content with life just the way it was. The thing that got to me was that I saw this in their children. The child's brain is like a sponge! Their minds are precious instruments. If the children only see or hear the "wrong way" to live their lives, then they tend not to shoot for much else. They hear and see rappers mainly, so they mostly want to live and be like rappers. They don't even realize that most of the rappers don't really have the lives they portray in the videos. The youngsters want to get money, but they don't really desire to earn it!

If too much television could make a person "stupid" then sometimes I could have been referred to as an "idiot," because I would catch myself wasting valuable time watching the television. Satan wants us all! If someone on the television would just tell the public the "pros and cons" to being famous, maybe they would just think about that more!?

In this neighborhood my sister was almost killed by some girl stabbed her in the head. Her "friends" were nowhere to be found. My sister just was a tough girl and she could defend herself. This older girl stepped to her with problems with her and she knew nothing about it. She just knocked the girl some feet into some bushes, with her fists. All the girl could think of doing was seriously cutting her in the face I guess!

For me it was time to seriously pray for her. At the Emergency Room the doctor told her that someone must have been praying for her, because the cut was so deep that she was almost brain dead. That must have been some serious prayer because right in the Emergency Room was the dumb girl. The police didn't even have to look for her. The police filed charges on her themselves for that. My sister was already a believer, but the first thing that I thought about doing was to pray for her. I do believe that God not only hears our prayers, but He also answers them!

My brother and his issues were manipulated by other people. He didn't even realize that they were taking advantage of him. This eventually got him in trouble with the law. The sad part was that by his mind being like that of a child, he really didn't even know any better!

I just felt so powerless in my little wheelchair! My sister got stabbed just for defending herself and my brother just used to get really upset and had psychotic episodes. I really don't know how many times the "slumlord" threatened to kick us out as a result of my brother "going off." He was a nasty man! It had to be God that kept us from being evicted with no place else to go. This place was crappy for me too, but still I didn't want to get forced out. Actually it was the worst of all places that I have lived! My brother used to keep to himself in the past. We wanted him to come out of his shell, but not like this! It just seemed as if my siblings were content with living back there. It must be some validity to what some people say, "People tend to be like who they're around."

Many, many, times, no one would be there for me! My little sister and brother had grown up and seemed to enjoy things just as they were. Their friends seemed to be more important to them than me, their big brother. Yes, this made me feel a little jealous! They wouldn't even take church seriously. By them being teenagers, they didn't really understand or fear God as much mind as I did. I was older and understood how important my faith was by now. In the past, at their ages, that was how I thought though.

Back then, to me there was just so much more time for that later! I just wasn't ready to fully surrender to God yet. Sometimes I wish that the light had been turned on inside of me before "this thing," but God knows exactly what He is doing. I am not mad. My siblings really made me feel as if to them, I wasn't that important. Sometimes I felt like I was just there holding place. But they needed me. They just didn't realize it. They never knew how much praying for them I did or how many times I sacrificed something that I needed to do to help them.

There were no new friends that visited me from day to day. Sometimes I felt like I was alone! All of my friends were far away from me. They were busy most of the time. They did have careers! There were times that some of them called me or just came by. One time my friend Latria came through from Durham. She was one of the only females that was a part of my crew. About fifty or more of my people showed up for the MS Walk twice just to support me. For two years straight by that time, they supported this cause. My people supported me and we had fun! It was almost like a mini-reunion. Lots more people that knew me wanted to show up, but for different reasons they were unable to make it.

My ex-girlfriend Tiffany is one of those friends that couldn't make it to the events. She did drive about an hour or so just to visit me though. When she came to visit in the past, I was in the hospital. But the last time that she visited me I had already moved to Greenville. In the past, when she came to visit me in the hospital, I lived in Scotland Neck. But it had been about three years since I had been to the hospital. By now being alone shouldn't bother me anymore. But truthfully, it did! Sometimes like I said before, "I could be in a crowded room and still feel alone." What I didn't realize or want to accept was that the lonely times were needed. Really, I couldn't be mad. The ugly word "hate" was really coming out of my mouth too much! I really didn't like this neighborhood sounds better.

The problem was that all I did was sit around waiting for my life to change. For a long time now socially I felt "bankrupt." It just hurt that not even my little brother and sister had time for me. If their lives were at stake and somebody asked them questions about Multiple Sclerosis, they wouldn't be able to answer them correctly. And they lived with someone who was living with it! This fact really had me frustrated.

Sometimes the mistakes they made maybe would have been avoided if they just talked to me or listened to me sometimes. I realized that they had to make some of those mistakes in order to learn. Being their big brother, because I loved them like they were my own children, I wanted them to skip those steps if they could. When growing up, many times I just wished that I had an older brother to talk with. Maybe he would protect me or give me some advice. If I did though, to be honest, I probably wouldn't have learned either until the mistake had already been made!

They seemed to have just had the mentality that, "If they couldn't beat them, they'd join them." You see for me, being "just like" someone else was never me. Me, I have always been more of an "individual." I understood the principle that, before I could lead I had to learn to follow.

But my way has always been unorthodox anyway. People sometimes tried to imitate me and not the other way around. My siblings though, seemed to be very busy doing absolutely nothing! They placed more value in their "friends" than on their family. They just tolerated me is how they made me feel. Really, when I think about it, back when they were small, they could've said the same things about me though. My focus was on the things that could better life for my entire family most of the times. When I was a teenager they were much younger than me anyway. My brother was ten years younger than me, and my sister was only born when I was fifteen. We did grow up differently. My grandma raised me, but my mom was did come over about every day. They always lived with our mother and their dad. My plans were to better the lives of my family and myself. This required me to be involved in something positive. I was always doing something dealing with the Boy Scouts or maybe it was something to do with sports. My siblings really never understood me. To them I was more like their uncle.

Moving right along, my mom at first had another job as a "temp" but it wasn't permanent either. One night while she worked third shift job as a "temp," my Cadillac, that I had gotten before I stopped driving, wouldn't start. The cab ride was kind of expensive, so this guy offered her a ride to work. His name was Demetric. By my mom not knowing him at all, my younger brother decided to ride with them. He just wanted to make sure that she was safe. Demetric and my mom ended up becoming friends. Later they developed a relationship. Once I got to know him, he did check out to be a great guy! He impressed me, because he was a genuinely good guy! There were times that I felt that my mom was lucky to have him around. Sometimes I even looked for him to come to our apartment. He was concerned about all of us, as if he had known us for years! He and my mom spent some time just playing cards with his people and doing other things in the beginning. It just so happened that as they talked, they discovered that Demetric had family back where we came from, Halifax County. His family and ours knew each other pretty well.

Once my mom finally landed a permanent job at Wal-Mart, time spent doing certain things with her new male friend had to decrease. She worked to Wal-Mart back when we lived in Halifax County, and she was qualified to do lots of things there. So she began to work a lot. When she worked there lots of things ended up taking a "back seat." She always went all out for pay at a job. The pay and the benefits there were wonderful! Her supervisors knew that she was a great asset to the job. She was elated to finally get a great permanent job! She was trying to get our family the hell out of where we lived!

A year of had gone by and we were still in the same neighborhood. It seemed as if we were stuck there. Either it was the car needing to be fixed or my brother did something stupid that came in the way of saving money. Money was always the thing that held us back. Not having much money held us back most of the time. Once she got her income tax check, my mom had to get another car. One was greatly needed, but a car payment was another bill! My family evidently had enough of my car by that time!? Personally my mind was on getting into a home that was better for me, but we did need another vehicle first. It was always one thing after another! My patience with just waiting was running very thin by that time. I was growing tired of the way my life had been going. Because of being fed up and frustrated, sometimes I felt like just screaming! Oh! No one could hear me scream, because it was inside that I screamed and cried! What I desperately needed and wanted was just somewhere else to live. A more accessible place for me would have been great!

This guy came into my life. Really, I don't know whether to call him my mentor, community based support guy, my brother, my friend, or what, but he got my confidence up to do what I had been wanting to do for a while now really. That was to just trust God and finally take the necessary steps to move out on my own. I was just so scared! His name was Garet Pahl. No, really just stepping out on faith had been on my mind for a while now. There were people in the past that have even tried to get me to go out on my own. There was just something that he made me realize that they couldn't. Now, he was from California and wasn't familiar with this disease. He decided to educate himself about it. On his quest to find out more about Multiple Sclerosis, he stumbled upon something that I had no knowledge of. It was a new program, provided by the MS Society that could aide me with improving my quality of life. It made me feel good, because he learned more about "this thing" without me having to tell him! It showed me that he really wanted to help me out!

The next step that we would take was to get me assigned to a care manager through the MS Society. Maybe she could help with our efforts to get me into more suitable apartment and neighborhood for me. The person that was provided for me name was Heather Brewer. The day that she visited my home she first checked out the apartment. She saw that the apartment and the neighborhood weren't ideal for anyone to live, especially a person with my "special" needs. Next the three of us sat down and came up with a plan.

Before meeting with Mrs. Brewer life for me seemed "dark." The light at the end of my "tunnel" had reappeared after meeting with her. This was just the metaphor that I always used to describe my view of life to myself. Sometimes it seemed as if I was traveling down a tunnel and the light was either far away and dim or close and the light was bright. "Far away and dim" meant that things weren't going so well. "Close and bright" meant that things were better and I was optimistic again. We came up with a plan. An escape plan you might call it. With them backing me, I applied to "The Life House of Greenville" for an apartment, a single room apartment. "The Life House" was for people with physical handicaps and their care givers, not whole families. It was based on their incomes also. The thought of living alone had left me with mixed feelings. On one hand I felt so sure that I can do this and on the other I was unsure. In my mind I just believed that God would be there with me and that somehow, someway, everything would work out.

My therapist told me that she didn't think that I should live alone yet. I was still determined to do it when my name came up on the waiting list. Once again I called the prophetess to tell me if God had wanted me to go through with it or not. I couldn't reach her at any of the numbers that I had for her. So what I did was to seriously pray and seek God for answers as to what I should do. One day, after praying earlier that morning, a solution to my problem just popped into my mind! I was to "Go back to where I started from and begin again." I kept what had happened to myself, as usual. It had to have been The Holy Spirit that whispered that idea to me. My pastor did tell us one day in church that we need to stop referring to The Holy Spirit as "something." Not long after that my mom really began to look aggressively for somewhere else to live. She knew from a conversation we had one day that I desperately wanted to live somewhere that was handicap accessible. I was feeling very frustrated, tired, and discouraged. She knew how I had been feeling ever since we left Barrett Place Apartments. Then one day while we were at church my pastor mentioned that the church had decided to help people who were hurting right here at home. She meant here in the good ole U.S.A! There were applications that could be gotten at the church. The monies would be awarded to only five people who the committee would choose to receive KCC stimulus checks.

You see at that time the economy was hurting, because of the "recession" that the country had found itself in. People had lost their jobs, homes, and for some even more than that. Some schools even were closed due to their budgets not having enough money in them to even operate. Because of families not being able to afford how and where they lived, school and classroom sizes changed and everything. President Barrack Obama was trying as hard as he could to help this nation. He did say that we all have to play our part to help fix this country's problems. He said that during his campaign. The day that he made history as the United States first African-American President, I turned thirty years old. His entire campaign was based on his promises of change. I don't know, but after hearing his Inauguration Speech, I just got this warm feeling inside!

Well, my mom applied for the help and was one of those people who were awarded the help! The church decided to go ahead and award twenty-five applicants instead of the five recipients that were initially supposed to get it. There were about two-hundred or so applicants. The church bought one family an entire home! With the money awarded to my mom we got caught up with any bill that we had as far as rent and light bill went.

Once we got caught up with the bills we began to hunt for another place to live. Getting away from that neighborhood, Mr. Fleet, and his "slumlord" mentality, was on our minds heavily. He wasn't really concerned about the people, but mainly the money. We applied and applied for different apartments and kept getting denied housing. One morning I just thought about what the idea that The Holy Spirit had whispered to me. Immediately, I gave Barrett Place Apartments a phone call. They had only one handicap accessible apartment open, so we went to fill out an application. This is where I started. He must have literally meant to "Go back to where I started!" I claimed that the open one was for us. The Holy Spirit did tell me to stay with my mom? We waited for an entire week! When they did call us they said that we didn't get that apartment either. For some reason, everything just didn't check out. When we lived there, we were excellent tenants. So, there just had to be another reason!

# "My World of Isolation"

I spend most of my days alone thinking, wondering, praying that what I believe, will manifest itself into a reality that never fails. Knowing that if it shall fail it HAD to be for my best because my "spirit man" is usually wiser than my "human flesh." *So why do I constantly ignore Him*!? I don't know! I just know that it is not because of my reputation. I mean it gets very lonely in my world of isolation.

Have you ever been to my world!? It's not a place for the weak. In my world only the strong survive. Trapped, getting used to a whole new way of life. You gotta keep it moving, no matter what! You have to stay alive. Sometimes you get lonely. Sometimes you may want to give in but inside you know that can't happen. In this world you might begin to feel empty because of your lack of participation. It happens sometimes in my world of isolation.

I know sometimes you feel like just giving in but you can't! You've come too far from where you started! The loneliness! The lack! Gotta keep pressing forward! Can't let the enemy win. You have the power to defeat him. Just look within. So in your world beware of the spirit of procrastination. It sometimes happens in your world of isolation.

*--Hiekaleez--*

# Chapter Eight

# Rescue Me!!

OVING BACK TO BARRETT PLACE Apartments was what I thought that the Holy Spirit meant, but I was so wrong! We found out that it was the "slum-lord" who was bad mouthing us to the other housing facilities. He was spiteful and just wanted to keep us in that neighborhood. What he said about us is what stopped us from moving! He "trumped" up the charges. He really got mad with the fact that we got an attorney from the church to help us! He even went so far as to lying about us being bad tenants. The landlord and my brother really made the past three years the worst in my life! He had "lied" to the church about how much money we owed him. He went on even further to bring up the damages that my brother caused. I mainly think that he didn't care too much for my brother. Really to me, my brother was one of my main problems too! So, we did qualify for the other apartment! It wasn't our credit after-all! It was a lie when we were told that they made a mistake from the other apartments. They told us that they didn't mean to tell us that we had been approved. We had already put in applications for other handicapped accessible apartments and everything!

I was just so sure that the idea that popped into my head came from the Holy Spirit. It seemed that at the time everyone checked our credit. We still had the problem of this "slumlord" interfering. Because of certain past issues, our credit wasn't good enough to move somewhere else. The entire country was in a deficit, and had bad credit. "If we didn't pay our rent, well then just evict us," is what I thought! In my heart of hearts, I just knew that we were going to move some place! God said in His word that, "He will never leave us nor would He forsake us," so there was no way or reason to doubt Him now! When my mom told a lady from the church that was on the committee that awarded the stimulus monies about this "slum-lord," the church just stepped in to help. The church set us up with an attorney, but the hateful and mean landlord just hooked up his records in a way that made him look good. Once again we were facing eviction with nowhere to go. From His Word, I learned that God can't lie, and He won't fail me. It would only be a minute before He steps in now. We only had ten days before we would be homeless. All of our things will be locked away and all! The only things that I could do were to pray and hope.

One morning while listening to the "Ricky Smiley" Morning Show someone was on and they said something about God loving situations that had our "backs against the walls." He loves it when we are totally dependent on Him. Usually every morning I listen to Steve Harvey, but for some reason, that morning I just turned from 95.5 to 92.1! Both of them gave me the laughs that I needed. For me it was kind of like therapy. Most mornings I woke up to Steve Harvey at 6 a.m to hear his encouraging words and jokes. Reading his book, *Act Like A Lady, Think Like A Man,* let me know that my ways weren't so wrong after all! I always had a burning desire to be all the man that he talked about in his book. I was glad when he broke our simplicity down to women. To get this though, I believe the first step a person must take is to be "a man." My pastor did say and I agree that, "You're a male or female by birth, and a man or woman by choice." The ages really don't matter much.

A phone call came in later that night and the person on the phone was someone from my church. He told me that one of the other members was telling him of me and my situation. He asked them for my number and gave me a call. This is what all that he told me anyway! He didn't mention any names, but mine. We just talked for a couple of hours that evening. Before we hung up he started asking me some questions about my finances. We had just talked about lots of other things over the phone. To me the questions about my finances were kind of personal. They just seemed intrusive and nosey. It is not in my nature to be mean though. "Since he was from Koinonia maybe he knew somebody who could help us," is what I thought. So of course, I told him. It was funny, because we had never even met before! It was something about him that made me open up to him and tell him things that I usually don't tell people. Once we hung up I just thought nothing of it. I just thought that he was just a nice guy from my church, a new friend of mine maybe? My first name, "Jermain" does mean "friend" after all!? Because he was a "Koinonia man," the phone conversation was not unordinary. "He was just being nice," I thought.

The next morning before lunch time, someone called me that was from a housing facility. This person told to me that we had already been approved for an apartment in the housing complex in which they were a manager. The deposit and the first month's rent were already taken care of. When I asked him, "Who arranged all of this?" he responded that he didn't know. All he knew was that he had instructions that were left on his desk to call me. I was so happy! No one at the church seemed to know my friend from the other night that called me. I just wanted to ask him if he was responsible for the good news that I had just received. All I wanted to do was thank him if he was responsible for it! The man never told me his name either. Since nobody took the credit for this blessing, I knew that it was all God! Sometimes just the thought of it gives me the chills. This has happened to me before, now that I think about it!? "God has done it, again," is what I said to myself! Whenever "my back is against the wall," He always steps right in and saves the day! All that I could do was just praise Him, and tell Him, "Thank you."

We moved in a week before Thanksgiving. My mom did say that by Thanksgiving we would be moving! We just enjoyed our new home. My cousin Monte got married to my friend's Willie's younger sister, Kacee, which was kind of awkward! I only said that because no one saw this before. After some time of them just dating, they announced that they were getting married. I couldn't be happier! I knew that a guy like him would be a "great catch!" One thing about it is that when a "Hieke" man gets married, he stays married! My uncle Jimmy has been married to his wife for over fifty years! His son, Jimmy Hieke, jr. and his uncle, Jemerald, have been married ever since I can remember too! She grew up with her mother and father, and they have been married for over thirty years. So my cousin's marriage was actually going to work! They had lots of people to learn from on how to make it work!

My cousin Monte first asked me to be his best man. We were close, but when we were in our teens, we grew a little apart socially. We weren't around each other like we were when we were younger, so I just thought that he was going to get someone else or something. His fiancé at the time, Kacee Hardy, wanted me to do a poem for them at their wedding. I was excited to do that! When he asked me to be his best-man, doubt crept in. In the beginning, for some reason, I doubted myself too much. When I sent Kacee a text message on her phone about my doubts of my ability to be his best-man, she told me that Monte really, really wanted me to do it! My eyes immediately began to water. I just got even more excited, because I knew that he really deserved to be happy. My cousin over the recent years had gone through a lot. Being an important part of one of the happiest moments in his life just had me in tears!

They were getting married one week before Christmas. Once again I was one of my boy's best-man! The first time was for my friend Andre, and now for my cousin, Monte. Monte wasn't just one of my boys, he was also my blood. When we were small, people thought we were brothers. We dressed alike. Whatever he wore in red, I wore in blue. We both loved his two sons and his mom was my favorite aunt. My entire family already liked his fiancé. To me, she was already my family. Her brother was like a brother to me and her mom was like my god-mother or something! So our two families were already intertwined.

The week after their wedding was Christmas. By the time the Spring Semester started, I applied for a tutoring position and a position as a G.E.D Instructor at Pitt Community College. To me it didn't matter which I was hired to do. With both of my applications, I attached my resume. The main things that were on my resume were the positions that I had as a tutor in the subjects of English and History. Also, I had on the resume that I was a G.E.D Instructor too. Of course, they checked my references for both positions. After they checked my references, it came up that I did a great job! They called me in for an interview. Without really interviewing me, they told me that they really would love it if I would be a G.E.D Instructor and tutor. They wanted me to tutor at Pitt Community College on Mondays and Wednesdays in addition to being an instructor for the G.E.D Classes on Tuesdays and Thursdays at the church. See, I had forgotten all about the fact that at Koinonia Christian Center Church, G.E.D Classes were held. I had no idea they were through the community college though.

After about a year or so of doing a great job, they asked me to take the position as supervisor to the tutors and the G.E.D Instructors at P.C.C. Before they could officially pay me the required salary, I would have to go back to school to get a Master's Degree. That was a goal of mine anyway! They were going to pay for me to get it and pay me while I went to school. All of this had to be God! In the *Bible,* it does say in 1 Corinthians 2:9 that "Eyes have not seen, nor ear heard, nor have entered into the heart of man; the things which God has prepared for those who love Him." I was so, so happy that it made me cry! Now all of that praying, alone time, and just pressing on no matter what was beginning to pay off. Of course, God being God, had lots more for me.

While I was taking Graduate Classes to get my Master's Degree at East Carolina University, one of my classmates came up to me and asked me to speak to her students. She was a nursing student, and she needed to bring in something like a film or just something visual for her project. She just wanted me to talk about Multiple Sclerosis and how it has affected my life. I love to talk. I told the students a few things about my battle with "this thing" and my faith in God. In my talk, I told the students that without my faith in God I think I would have just thrown in the towel! When I finished my testimony they all just cried. Well as I was leaving the entire class thought that I should just speak to some people as a motivational speaker or something. I just told them that right now I was in Graduate School to get my Master's Degree in Social Work. I went on to tell them to not ever give up on their goals in life! They were mixed in ethnicity and beliefs. Some of them wanted to come to Koinonia Christian Center Church to witness my church for themselves! Of course, I just told them all that they were all welcomed to come and worship with us on Sunday.

It was about two years later before I finally got my Master's. I was thirty-three by then, but at least I did get it! Before "this thing," I had planned to have my Doctorate in something by age thirty! My goals to achieve my dream hadn't died, it was just delayed. The entire time that I was in Graduate School though, I tutored and was a G.E.D Instructor at the community college. Because of my course-load, I was only part-time though. My life was quite busy. I had class twice a week. I tutored and instructed a G.E.D class. The entire time, I also had physical therapy twice a week and papers to write with reading to do. Believe it or not there was still plenty of time for me to go to church, Bible Study, and read my bible. See, I just devoted two hours early in the morning, while no one was stirring, to seek God and pray. Maybe that's why I always had enough energy to do all of the other things!? Really what I needed to do was focus more on my social life, because the one that I had was pitiful!

The entire time that I was doing all of the other things like I said, I was taking Physical Therapy. It was time for me to just finally step out there on my own and get my own place. My name on the waiting list at The Life House of Greenville had been passed. Really, by now I didn't want that anyway! There was this one bedroom, nice apartment near Pitt Community College available. It was nice and it was ready for the handicapped. My motorized power chair and my wheelchair was still how I got around at the time. I did just about everything just fine from the chairs by then anyway. At that time it had been about ten years since I actually walked anywhere. My family was still a little reluctant to agree with my move out on my own. But I just had faith that it would all be okay! Well anyway, I was approved for an apartment and before it got hot, I was moving in.

# "Who Got Me!?"

**Who got me when I am hurting?**
**Who got me when I cry?**
**I know who got me.**
**It's my God in the sky.**
Really, He's all around me
Do I need to tell you how I know?
In His book it is written.
He loves me. The Bible tells me so.
**I spent too much time running.**
**I mean really, where was I trying to go?**
**He knew this, but He saved me.**
**It's Him I am getting to know.**
In His word it says He knew me
While I was still in my mother's womb.
He stepped right in to provide light
So that this flower can bloom.
**I know who got me when I'm hurting.**
**I know who got me when I cry.**
**I know who got me.**
**It's my God in the sky.**

*-- Hiekaleez--*

# Chapter Nine

# Socially Restored

THE DAY CAME THAT SPRING, about two weeks before Easter that I would be living in my own place. Of course, it was an accessible apartment. It was huge and I was kind of scared! The MS Society gave me a check to buy some things for my new home. The check was for $2500.00. Some members from my church gave me most of the furniture that I needed. My tuition for Graduate School had already been taken care of. That money went into my bank account until I figured out what I was going to do with it after I paid my tithes. Some of my friends came over to decorate at my apartment my "house warming" party. Furnishing my apartment was taken care of by just some of the people, mainly females, who I already knew. They all brought me different things to hook my apartment up with. And my mom came by to put in her little efforts!

Once my apartment was all set up to start with, living on my own was a huge adjustment for me. I was living alone for the first time. Now living alone had to be done with "this thing" in my life. But I did always plan to live alone, so what was the problem!? This was another dream of mine. Being "independent" was not what I wanted. It was what I craved! I just had to "man up," as they say! Now it was my turn to finally see if I could "cut it!" If someone else can do it then so could I! Well, God is leading me and with that fact, I am never really alone. My life had gotten so busy that I was hardly ever home anyway! Either I was at a library studying, at the church, or something. I was so busy, because for years I was inactive. Really, there wasn't anyone at home waiting for me, so being to these places at least kept people around me!

It had been almost ten years now since I had a "girl-friend!" There was no one to share my spare time with, like a girlfriend or anything. I did see plenty of females that were both attractive and smart, but my problem was me! I just couldn't get past my past! It was said that, "You are only allowed one true love in your life-time." That statement can't be true! It was just that I had already been "in-love" twice and I love them both still! You see to me being "in-love" is more of a temporary thing than if you "love" someone. You can "love" someone and still be "in-love" with them, but you could also just be "in-love" with someone and never really love them though. Although the two females were totally different on the outside, their inner-selves were beautiful! I met Farrah just by chance during my first year at Central. Her friend Deya, that I was introduced to by my friend Jade, brought that on. We were done, but at the end of my college career, Tiffany came in. We almost "never was" either. Both of those stories were like wow! They must have been special to me, because not every girl is brought home to meet your family. Quantity was never my thing, just quality!

There were many females that I was cool with in my past though. I've always been curious about females. Back in college, it was my "home-girls" that schooled me on females. I was dumb to that, because who could tell me more about females and how they think than females!? It was mainly when my friends Ebonie, Elana, and Tamara who sat outside the dorm with me, back in college, that gave me these lessons. When it came to the books, I could "hold it down," but when it came to the opposite sex, I was just "clueless!" Most of the girls that I hung with were gorgeous and smart too! A lot of my boys just thought that I was trying to get up with these girls sexually. To me they were just my friends. Maybe just listening to them was not what most of the other guys were thinking about. They might have wanted more. I won't lie and say that there weren't times that my thoughts were more than friendly. But when I thought about it more, it wasn't worth risking messing up what we had.

No one ever said anything to me as far as being interested in me or anything. So I just thought nothing of it. No, but really females were always just on my mind! My goal since I lost my ability to walk was to learn to live and move forward with my life! The devil stole that from me and I want it back! Who wants me now? Can I be the man that any of them would want? What do I have to offer? These were just a few of the questions that I asked myself sometimes. This all came from me still being so insecure and these were only a few of my insecurities! Inside I felt broken, inadequate, and as if I was not what women wanted! It was just that my past loves raised my expectations of a great mate so high! No, because now my life had changed. I just knew that my best days hadn't even happened yet. As long as I had faith and God, it was always possible that I would be in a serious relationship again. Maybe in His plan, I had already met the mate that He had for me!

The radio is on 104.3 and the DJ announces that the upcoming portion is dedicated to the lovers. I look to the right of me and then to the left. There's no one there. It had been a while since I shared that feeling with someone special. It's a "trip" when you realize that you have no other person to spend some time with. It has been a long time since "this thing" seriously changed my life. Most of the time listening to my favorite musician, "Musiq-Soul child," just brought up tears. In most of his songs it was like he was in my head or something. Whenever one of his songs was on, immediately a thought of my last girlfriend, Tiffany, comes up. Maybe it was because we went to one of his shows together one time. She surprised me with a ticket. This was my first experience in attending a famous singer's show. She knew that I was a huge fan of his, so she just decided to take me. We even sang one of his songs together one day in her car. Maybe the memories of some of our experiences together were why my feelings for her were so strong!

Some people say that the reason just why I can't get past her might be that she was my last girlfriend before "this thing" (Multiple Sclerosis) infiltrated my body. But what I felt for her was more than that! She visited me in the hospital and she didn't even have to! I guess I could at least try to move on, because the feeling just might not be mutual. And I can accept that. It was just that she knew me in the past when physically, I was healthy. Sometimes it just seems like I'm not good enough of a "catch" to the females. I only needed just one. I needed someone to laugh, cry, hurt, worship, and to grow old with!

There were a few girls that I met who would've been great for me though. My confidence was gone for some time, and this female just popped into my life. She possessed the qualities that made her attractive to me. She was attractive, independent, and smart just to name a few! Her name was Burgundy. It was her voice that grabbed me at first. I also just loved her name. It was original to me and that's what I liked. She made me begin to believe that maybe someone would come into my life as my girl-friend. My "condition" may have been an issue though! Every time that I scheduled a ride using Pitt Area Transit, I hoped that she would be the driver. When she would talk to me, with her light voice, she would call me "Sweetie!" She even told others at her job that I was cute and all. Some of the other female drivers told that's what she said about me. She seemed like the ideal girl for me, but we just became friends. I just don't think that most females wanted to give me a chance. It might have just been me! I mean she already had a son, and I met him once. When she took me to the library and the barbershop, I could tell that she might not have been my type through our conversations on the way! Maybe when she just smiled and was really nice to me, she was just being polite and didn't want to hurt my feelings!?

This other girl that went to high school with me, and I had known her and her family for most of my life, caught my eye. Well, in the past I did have a small 'crush' on her, but like I said before, I was "scared of girls" when I was in school. She and I were friends, but now we are all grown up. By then though, my life had changed. She also had all of the qualities that I was looking for. Her nickname was 'Shaun.' Just like Tiffany and Burgundy, when I just told her of my thoughts of her, she didn't tell me that I didn't have a chance with her either. She just said what all of the others said, " If it's in God's plans well then just maybe."

One Sunday morning I was just having church at home, because I felt kind of weak. I came across a verse in the bible that just "stuck out like a sore thumb." *The Holy Bible* says in Matthew 6:33 that people should "Seek first the kingdom of God and His righteousness, and all these things shall be added to you." So I won't worry about being in a relationship with a female. First, I will just seek God and let him decide. I decided to just do what *The Holy Bible* said. That following Tuesday, when I checked my mail, there was a letter from East Carolina University Nursing Program in it. A great opportunity was presented to me. I didn't know whether I would take it or not. What am I to do now!? My problem with making decisions had always been that I think too much. With this new news from this letter, I decided to do just what God had told me back in the past. "Trust God with all of my heart, and lean not unto my own understanding" (Proverbs 3:5, 6).

# "Love, Where You At!?"

Love, Where you at!? I've been looking for you, but just can't seem
To find you. I used to know your number, but you must have changed it.
I just wish you would call mine because it's still the same.
I just sit here day by day and wait for my phone to ring;
Hoping that it be you on the other end telling me that you just got
Lost for a while and that you're on your way back to me.
It's driving me to just give up and pray that God shows you the
Way back home where you belong. I try but I can't give up because
I know that the phone is gonna ring!
Love, where you at!?

*--Hiekaleez--*

# "When it's All Said and Done"

What do you want them to say
When it's all said and done?
That your life was worth living!?
That they hate that you're gone!?

When it's all said and done
Can you say that you tried!?
To live a good life
With God as your guide!?

Before you left this life
Did you try your very best?
Use the talents you were blessed with
Nothing more, nothing less!

If you answered yes to the questions I asked
Then you've already won!
Relax, Jesus loves you always;
Now that it's all said and done.

*--Hiekaleez--*

# Chapter Ten

# This Thing

MULTIPLE SCLEROSIS IS A DEBILITATING chronic disease of the Central Nervous System. By MS being a chronic illness, as of yet, there is no cure. The causes Multiple Sclerosis still is a mystery to scientists, but each year new information is discovered. It is for this reason that I call the disease itself, a coward! I read a book once about different theories as to what may cause MS. The theory that stuck out to me the most was the one that suggests that maybe it is because I have never had the Chicken Pox. What I thought was that maybe my body is just attacking itself mistaking MS for the Chicken Pox. It is an auto-immune disease! Another thing that I thought could have been may be the reason for me getting MS, was because I have had many head injuries that weren't really that serious at the time. Some of them came from just playing ball, an accident that I was involved in, or maybe it came from this once that this coward hit me in the head. None of these theories have been proven though, but as my friend says, "Oh well!" Just maybe it was slowly infecting my brain because all of those things together!? I don't know, but there is no need for me to cry now, huh!? As they say, "It is what it is!"

Symptoms of having MS usually are experienced by certain people between 20 and 40 years of age. A diagnosis is easily looked past, because it is not easy to recognize without certain tests being done. These tests can be a magnetic resonance imaging (MRI), an evoked potentials check (EPs), and a Spinal Tap to check for Spinal fluids to confirm the analysis, and a few more. I had all those tests! This disease is still kind of new. Let me correct myself, because Multiple Sclerosis has been around for some time now. Not until recently have there have new developments. People who have Multiple Sclerosis (MS) have the same life expectancy as those who are living without it. The yearly cost for MS is in the billions of dollars.

Scientists have recorded MS cases in younger children and in elderly adults. But before the age of 15 and after the age of 60, experiencing the symptoms of MS is very rare. Whites are more likely to develop MS than people of other races. MS affects women more than men in general. In people who get symptoms of MS later in their lives, the gender ratio is more balanced. Statistics on MS, say that almost 250,000 to 350,000 people have been diagnosed with it in the United States. This information suggests that the numbers are about 200 new cases a week. So this is just the number of people who already know that they have MS. There may be more people than that who don't even know yet! Also in Dr. Arthur Schoenstadt's observations, he noted that location is also a factor. People who live in temperate climates, such as those in the northern United States, Canada, and Europe, are five times more likely to develop MS than people that live in tropical regions.

Having Multiple Sclerosis has really been frustrating for me. "This thing" has taken away a lot from me physically, but I also learned a lot. I have learned lots about people and life in general. Most of these things that I used to hear about, but I took them for granted. It has taken away my ability to walk, stand, and just to be independent.

Never in a million years, did I think that this could happen to me! My experiences with "this thing" have been both humbling while also really been like a test for me. There were many times that it has caused me to feel lonely and powerless. But there was a point that all of the crying just had to stop!

With President Obama approving stem cell research, a cure for Multiple Sclerosis is clearly within our grasp. Already, I already feel like my healing is right here, right now! My faith in God has allowed me to remain so optimistic. From reading certain books and with my faith in God, I found my purpose in life. I switched from being a "victim" of this cowardly disease to realizing that I am a "victor." The devices that satan has tried to use to destroy me, God is using to bring Him the glory. So my enemies, being satan and through him Multiple Sclerosis, are already defeated. What the enemy meant for bad, God is using for my good. I can remember when "Ma Hardy" said to me once this certain verse from *The Holy Bible*, it was 1 Corinthians 2:9. It reads. Because an "Eye has not seen, nor ear heard, nor have entered into the heart of man the things which God has prepared for those who love Him." I am just a man, put here for the purpose of "mankind."

# "The Game of Life"

You're dealt a hand in life.
This I feel is true.
Sometimes you're dealt one.
Sometimes you're dealt two.
You're dealt one when young.
The other when you're old.
The red cards when you're hot.
The black cards when you're cold.
It all depends on if you play right.
Whether you win or lose is up to you.
When playing the game of life.

*--Hiekaleez--*